EASY WEDDING PLANNING PLUS

From America's Top Wedding Experts

Elizabeth & Alex Lluch
Authors of Over 3 Million Books Sold!

WS Publishing Group
San Diego, California

EASY WEDDING PLANNING PLUS
7TH EDITION

Written by Elizabeth & Alex Lluch
America's Top Wedding Experts

Published by WS Publishing Group
San Diego, California 92119
© Copyright 2009 by WS Publishing Group

Floral Descriptions Written and Researched by:
Joan Hahn Perilla
Partner, Public Relations Marketing, Inc.
Marketing Consultant to the Flower Council of Holland

Design by:
Sarah Jang, WS Publishing Group

For Inquiries:
Log on to www.WSPublishingGroup.com
E-mail info@WSPublishingGroup.com

Printed in China and Korea
ISBN 13: 978-1-934386-46-0

THE WEDDING OF

Chris Mellors

&

Tonya Gossen

WHO WILL BE MARRIED ON

AT

A SPECIAL THANKS TO OUR CONTRIBUTING PHOTOGRAPHERS

PHOTO CREDITS:
Cover Photograph: Karen French
Dividers & Pockets: Photo credit appears next to each photograph.

Tina Carlone
Tina Carlone Photography
Los Angeles, CA
(323) 669-8455
E-mail: tina@tinacarlone.com
www.tinacarlone.com

Miguel and Jennifer Fairbanks
Fairbanks and Fairbanks
Wedding Photography
P.O. Box 903
Summerland, CA 93067
(805) 565-9119
E-mail: miguelfairbanks@aol.com
www.fairbanksandfairbanks.com

Karen French
Karen French Photography
8351 Elmcrest Lane
Huntington Beach, CA 92646
(800) 734-6219
E-mail: info@karenfrenchphotography.com
www.karenfrenchphotography.com

Andy Marcus
Fred Marcus Photography
245 West 72nd Street
New York, NY 10023
(212) 873-5588
E-mail: info@fredmarcus.com
www.fredmarcus.com

Larry Monet
Photography by Monet
3708 Sixth Avenue
San Diego, CA 92103
(888) 827-7725
E-mail: info@photographybymonet.com
www.photographybymonet.com

Ryan and Carrie Phillips
Ryan Phillips Photography
P.O. Box 1636
Thousand Oaks, CA 91358
(805) 405-2131
E-mail: carrie@ryanphillipsphotography.com
www.ryanphillips.com

SOTA Weddings
SOTA Dzine INC.
2724 Dorr Ave. Bay #3
Fairfax, VA 22031
(703) 645-0900
E-mail: info@sotaphotography.com
www.sotaweddings.com

Wedding Solutions
7290 Navajo Rd.
Suite 207
San Diego, CA 92119
www.weddingsolutions.com

CONTENTS

INTRODUCTION 7

SWEET MEMORIES 9

WEDDING EVENTS AT A GLANCE..13

WEDDING PLANNING CHECKLIST 17

BUDGET ANALYSIS..25

CEREMONY 35

UNIQUE WEDDING IDEAS..47

ATTIRE 49

PHOTOGRAPHY 63

VIDEOGRAPHY...77

STATIONERY...85

ADDRESSING INVITATIONS...107

RECEPTION 109

MUSIC (CEREMONY AND RECEPTION)..131

BAKERY 139

FLOWERS 145

CONTENTS

POPULAR WEDDING FLOWERS..163

DECORATIONS 193

TRANSPORTATION 195

RENTAL ITEMS...199

GIFTS 209

PARTIES..211

MISCELLANEOUS...213

TIMELINES 225

WEDDING TRADITIONS 235

DO'S AND DON'TS 239

WEDDING PARTY RESPONSIBILITIES..243

WHO PAYS FOR WHAT 249

WEDDING FORMATIONS 251

THINGS TO BRING 257

WEDDING PLANNING CALENDAR 259

EASY HONEYMOON PLANNING...273

TELL US ABOUT YOUR WEDDING...321

INTRODUCTION

DEAR BRIDE AND GROOM,

CONGRATULATIONS ON YOUR ENGAGEMENT! You must be very excited to have found that special person with whom you will share the rest of your life. And you must be looking forward to what will be one of the happiest days of your life—your wedding! Planning a wedding can be fun and exciting, but it can also be very stressful; that is why Wedding Solutions created *Easy Wedding Planning Plus*.

Easy Wedding Planning Plus contains over 100 worksheets, checklists, timelines and comparison charts to keep you organized and on top of your plans. This new edition features a beautiful new look as well as updated wedding planning information on all aspects of the wedding planning process.

Easy Wedding Planning Plus begins with a detailed wedding planning checklist containing everything you need to do or consider when planning your wedding and the best time frame in which to accomplish each activity. Many of the items in the checklist are followed by the page number(s) where those items are explained within the book.

The checklist is followed by a comprehensive and detailed budget analysis. This section lists all the expenses that are typically incurred in a wedding, as well as the percentage of the total budget that is typically spent in each category. Next to each expense item is the page number where you can find detailed information regarding each item.

The budget analysis is followed by a detailed description of each item in the budget including: Options, Things to Consider, Questions to Ask, Things to Beware Of, Tips to Save Money, and Price Ranges. Our clients find this format to be both informative and easy to use, and we know you will too!

Following the detailed description of each item in the budget are wedding timelines for your wedding party as well as your service providers. Use these timelines to keep everyone on schedule.

Next is a short chapter on wedding traditions, explaining the symbolic meaning and historical significance of some of the more common wedding traditions, and a list of "Do's" and "Don'ts" when planning your wedding.

INTRODUCTION

We have also included a list of responsibilities for each member of your wedding party and a breakdown of who pays for what. We also provide traditional formations for the ceremony, processional, recessional and receiving line for both Jewish and Christian weddings as well as traditional seating arrangements at the reception.

Easy Wedding Planning Plus also has descriptions and color photographs of ninety popular wedding flowers. We hope this helps you make the appropriate flower selection and coordinate your overall color scheme.

Lastly, we have included a section to help you prepare for your honeymoon. This section will help you choose your ideal destination and develop a comprehensive budget as you plan for the vacation of your dreams. Also included are detailed packing lists, information on international travel, lists of useful resources and more.

Additional organizational features include thirteen full-color dividers. These dividers are located at the beginning of each section so you can find the information you need quickly and easily. These dividers feature beautiful photographs of weddings from around the country. Refer to these photos for inspiration and ideas.

At the back of the book you will find a folder with two pockets to store contracts, receipts, magazine articles and other loose paperwork.

This edition also includes *The Ultimate Fashion & Beauty Guide*. This illustrated pocket-sized guide contains everything you need to know to look your very best on your wedding day. It includes helpful guidelines on wedding dress styles, accessories, makeup, hair and skin care, as well as a complete section for the groom. You can be sure that you look your most stunning on your special day with the help of this guide.

We are confident that you will enjoy planning your wedding with the help of *Easy Wedding Planning Plus*. Also, if you know other Options, Things to Consider, Tips to Save Money, or anything else that you would like to see included in this book, please write to us at: WS Publishing Group; 7290 Navajo Road, Suite 207; San Diego, California 92119. We will include your ideas and suggestions in our next printing. We listen to brides and grooms like you—that is why Wedding Solutions has become the best-selling publisher of wedding planners!

Sincerely,

Elizabeth H. Lluch

SWEET MEMORIES

THE MOMENT SOMEONE SPECIAL PROPOSES is a memory that is cherished forever. The story will be told over and over, to friends, family, children, and grandchildren ...

How was your proposal special? Did he plan an elaborate scheme, or was it a simple, romantic display of his love for you? Did you propose to him? Every proposal is special and unique. You will have it forever, in your mind and in your heart.

Use the following pages to record that precious moment so the two of you can relive your memories together.

Answer the questions as you remember them. Let your words reflect the memory of each moment. Come back to these pages often as you plan your wedding. Reading about the day you got engaged will help to keep your romantic thoughts alive as you plan the event that will bind the two of you together for the rest of your lives!

THE PROPOSAL

Date: April 24 2010
Time: 11 Am
Location: Pacific Shores
Proposed by: Walk on the beach.

He/she said/did:

You said/did:

Then we did/went to:

My parents' reaction was:

_____
_____
_____
_____
_____
_____

His/her parents' reaction was:

_____
_____
_____
_____
_____
_____

My best friend's reaction was:

_____
_____
_____
_____
_____
_____

His/her best friend's reaction was:

_____
_____
_____
_____
_____
_____

NOTES

WEDDING EVENTS
AT A GLANCE

YOUR WEDDING WILL BE A CELEBRATION that will most likely span several different events. From the moment you get engaged to your last dance, your life will be filled with many special occasions.

Use the following worksheets to easily keep track of events, dates, locations, and contact information. Keeping these details in one place will help you plan ahead for each party and quickly reference important information.

Once you have finalized all of your events, make copies of these worksheets and distribute them to members of your wedding party, consultants, or vendors who would require this information.

WEDDING EVENTS AT A GLANCE

ENGAGEMENT PARTY DATE:

Engagement Party Time:

Engagement Party Location:

Contact Person: Phone Number:

Website: E-mail:

BRIDAL SHOWER DATE:

Bridal Shower Time:

Bridal Shower Location:

Contact Person: Phone Number:

Website: E-mail:

BACHELOR PARTY DATE:

Bachelor Party Time:

Bachelor Party Location:

Contact Person: Phone Number:

Website: E-mail:

BACHELORETTE PARTY DATE:

Bachelorette Party Time:

Bachelorette Party Location:

Contact Person: Phone Number:

Website: E-mail:

CEREMONY REHEARSAL DATE:

Ceremony Rehearsal Time:

Ceremony Rehearsal Location:

Contact Person: Phone Number:

Website: E-mail:

REHEARSAL DINNER DATE:

Rehearsal Dinner Time:

Rehearsal Dinner Location:

Contact Person: Phone Number:

Website: E-mail:

CEREMONY DATE:

Ceremony Time:

Ceremony Location:

Contact Person: Phone Number:

Website: E-mail:

RECEPTION DATE:

Reception Time:

Reception Location:

Contact Person: Phone Number:

Website: E-mail:

INFORMATION AT A GLANCE

VENDOR	Company	Contact Person	Phone #	Website/E-mail
Wedding Consultant				
Ceremony Site				
Officiant				
Reception Site				
Caterer				
Liquor Services				
Wedding Gown				
Tuxedo Rental				
Photographer				
Videographer				
Stationer				
Calligrapher				
Music: Ceremony				
Music: Reception				
Florist				
Bakery				
Decorations				
Ice Sculpture				
Party Favor				
Balloonist				
Transportation				
Rental & Supplies				
Gift Suppliers				
Valet Services				
Gift Attendant				
Rehearsal Dinner				

WEDDING PLANNING CHECKLIST

THE FOLLOWING WEDDING PLANNING CHECKLIST ITEMIZES everything you need to do or consider when planning your wedding and the best time frame in which to accomplish each activity.

As you can see, many of the items are prefaced by the page number(s) where they are explained in more detail within the book. This will help you find the information you need quickly.

This checklist assumes that you have at least nine months to plan your wedding. If your wedding is in less than nine months, just start at the beginning of the list and try to catch up as quickly as you can!

Use the boxes to the left of the items to check off the activities as you accomplish them. This will enable you to see your progress and help you determine what has been done and what still needs to be done.

WEDDING PLANNING CHECKLIST

NINE MONTHS AND EARLIER

PAGE

- ❑ Announce your engagement.

- ❑ Select a date for your wedding.

216   ❑ Hire a professional wedding consultant.

- ❑ Determine the type of wedding you want: location, formality, time of day, number of guests.

25-33   ❑ Determine budget and how expenses will be shared.

34   ❑ Develop a record-keeping system for payments made.

- ❑ Consolidate all guest lists: bride's, groom's, bride's family, groom's family, and organize:
  1) those who must be invited
  2) those who should be invited
  3) those who would be nice to invite

- ❑ Decide if you want to include children among guests.

35   ❑ Select and reserve ceremony site.

36   ❑ Select and reserve your officiant.

NINE MONTHS AND EARLIER (CONT.)

PAGE

109   ❑ Select and reserve reception site.

49-51   ❑ Select and order your bridal gown and headpiece.

- ❑ Determine color scheme.

67, 213   ❑ Send engagement notice with a photograph to your local newspaper.

14-15, 211, 259   ❑ Use the calendar provided to note all important activities: showers, luncheons, parties, get-togethers, etc.

- ❑ If ceremony or reception is at home, arrange for home or garden improvements as needed.

63   ❑ Select and book photographer.

- ❑ Order passport, visa, or birth certificate, if needed, for your honeymoon or marriage license.

244   ❑ Select maid of honor, best man, bridesmaids, and ushers (approximately one usher per 50 guests).

SIX TO NINE MONTHS BEFORE WEDDING

PAGE

246-247 ❑ Select flower girl and ring bearer.

❑ Give the *Wedding Party Responsibility Cards* to your wedding party. These cards are published by Wedding Solutions and are available at major book stores.

❑ Reserve wedding night bridal suite.

61 ❑ Select attendants' dresses, shoes, and accessories.

110 ❑ Select and book caterer, if needed.

131 ❑ Select and book ceremony musicians.

132 ❑ Select and book reception musicians or DJ.

60-62 ❑ Schedule fittings and delivery dates for yourself, attendants, and flower girl.

77 ❑ Select and book videographer.

145 ❑ Select and book florist.

FOUR TO SIX MONTHS BEFORE WEDDING

PAGE

209 ❑ Start shopping for each other's wedding gifts.

199 ❑ Reserve rental items needed for ceremony.

104 ❑ Finalize guest list.

85 ❑ Select and order wedding invitations, announcements, and other stationery such as thank-you notes, wedding programs, and seating cards.

95, 107 ❑ Address invitations or hire a calligrapher.

15, 212 ❑ Set date, time, and location for your rehearsal dinner.

106 ❑ Arrange accommodations for out-of-town guests.

❑ Start planning your honeymoon.

117 ❑ Select and book all miscellaneous services, i.e., gift attendant, valet parking, etc.

❑ Register for gifts.

52-53 ❑ Purchase shoes and accessories.

53 ❑ Begin to break in your shoes.

WEDDING PLANNING CHECKLIST

TWO TO FOUR MONTHS BEFORE WEDDING

PAGE

139   ❑ Select bakery and order wedding cake.

115, 127   ❑ Order party favors.

193   ❑ Select and order room decorations.

   ❑ Purchase honeymoon attire and luggage.

195   ❑ Select and book transportation for wedding day.

214   ❑ Check blood test and marriage license requirements.

   ❑ Shop for wedding rings and have them engraved.

   ❑ Consider having your teeth cleaned or bleached.

214   ❑ Consider writing a will and/or prenuptial agreement.

   ❑ Plan activities for out-of-town guests both before and after the wedding.

210   ❑ Purchase gifts for wedding attendants.

SIX TO EIGHT WEEKS BEFORE WEDDING

PAGE

85, 93   ❑ Mail invitations. Include accommodation choices and a map to assist guests in finding the ceremony and reception sites.

94, 104   ❑ Maintain a record of RSVPs and all gifts received. Send thank-you notes upon receipt of gifts.

53   ❑ Determine hairstyle and makeup.

53   ❑ Schedule to have your hair, makeup, and nails done the day of the wedding.

36-37, 141   ❑ Finalize shopping for wedding day accessories such as toasting glasses, ring pillow, guest book, etc.

   ❑ Set up an area or a table in your home to display gifts as you receive them.

213   ❑ Check with your local newspapers for wedding announcement requirements.

65   ❑ Have your formal bridal portrait taken.

213   ❑ Send wedding announcement and photograph to your local newspapers.

SIX TO EIGHT WEEKS BEFORE WEDDING (CONT.)

PAGE

221-223	❑ Check requirements to change your name and address on your driver's license, social security card, insurance policies, subscriptions, bank accounts, etc.
54	❑ Select and reserve wedding attire for groom, ushers, ring bearer, and father of the bride.
36	❑ Select a guest book attendant. Decide where and when to have guests sign in.
	❑ Mail invitations to rehearsal dinner.
214	❑ Get blood test and health certificate.
214	❑ Obtain Marriage License.
212	❑ Plan a luncheon or dinner with your bridesmaids. Give them their gifts at that time or at the rehearsal dinner.
236	❑ Find "something old, something new, something borrowed, something blue, and a sixpence (or shiny penny) for your shoe."
110-113 126, 130	❑ Finalize your menu, beverage, and alcohol order.

TWO TO SIX WEEKS BEFORE WEDDING

PAGE

	❑ Confirm ceremony details with your officiant.
61	❑ Arrange final fitting of bridesmaids' dresses.
60	❑ Have final fitting of your gown and headpiece.
145, 158-160	❑ Make final floral selections.
92, 212	❑ Finalize rehearsal dinner plans; arrange seating and write names on place cards, if desired.
226-229	❑ Make a detailed timeline for your wedding party.
230-233	❑ Make a detailed timeline for your service providers.
232-233	❑ Confirm details with all service providers, including attire. Give them copies of your wedding timeline.
	❑ Start packing for your honeymoon.
94, 105	❑ Finalize addressing and stamping announcements.

TWO TO SIX WEEKS BEFORE WEDDING (CONT.)

PAGE

256 ❑ Decide if you want to form a receiving line. If so, determine when and where to form the line.

❑ Contact guests who haven't responded.

❑ Pick up rings and check for fit.

74-76 ❑ Meet with photographer and confirm special photos you want taken.

77 ❑ Meet with videographer and confirm special events or people you want videotaped.

43, 131, 138 ❑ Meet with musicians and confirm music to be played during special events such as the first dance.

94, 104 ❑ Continue writing thank-you notes as gifts arrive.

61, 62 ❑ Remind bridesmaids and ushers of when and where to pick up their wedding attire.

53-54 ❑ Purchase the lipstick, nail polish, and any other accessories you want your bridesmaids to wear.

45-46 ❑ Determine ceremony seating for special guests. Give a list to the ushers.

92, 124 ❑ Plan reception room layout and seating with your reception site manager or caterer. Write names on place cards for arranged seating.

THE LAST WEEK

PAGE

60-62 ❑ Pick up wedding attire and make sure everything fits.

❑ Do final guest count and notify your caterer or reception site manager.

257-258 ❑ Gather everything you will need for the rehearsal and wedding day as listed in the *Wedding Party Responsibility Cards*.

244 ❑ Arrange for someone to drive the getaway car.

232-233 ❑ Review the schedule of events and last minute arrangements with your service providers. Give them each a detailed timeline.

❑ Confirm all honeymoon reservations and accommodations. Pick up tickets and traveler's checks.

❑ Finish packing your suitcases for the honeymoon.

104 ❑ Familiarize yourself with guests' names. It will help during the receiving line and reception.

❑ Notify the post office to hold mail while you are away on your honeymoon.

THE REHEARSAL DAY

PAGE

257 ❑ Review list of things to bring to the rehearsal as listed in the *Wedding Party Responsibility Cards*.

❑ Put suitcases in getaway car.

❑ Give your bridesmaids the lipstick, nail polish, and accessories you want them to wear for the wedding.

244 ❑ Give best man the officiant's fee and any other checks for service providers. Instruct him to deliver these checks the day of the wedding.

❑ Arrange for someone to bring accessories such as flower basket, ring pillow, guest book and pen, toasting glasses, cake cutting knife, and napkins to the ceremony and reception.

94, 244 ❑ Arrange for someone to mail announcements the day after the wedding.

199, 244 ❑ Arrange for someone to return rental items such as tuxedos, slip, and cake pillars after the wedding.

228-229 ❑ Provide each member of your wedding party with a detailed schedule of events/timelines for the wedding day.

45-46 ❑ Review ceremony seating with ushers.

THE WEDDING DAY

PAGE

258 ❑ Review list of things to bring to the ceremony as listed in the *Wedding Party Responsibility Cards*.

❑ Give the groom's ring to the maid of honor.

❑ Give the bride's ring to the best man.

228-229 ❑ Simply follow your detailed schedule of events.

❑ Relax and enjoy your wedding!

NOTES

BUDGET ANALYSIS

THIS COMPREHENSIVE BUDGET ANALYSIS HAS BEEN DESIGNED to provide you with all the expenses that can be incurred in any size wedding, including such hidden costs as taxes, gratuities, stamps, and other "items" that can easily add up to thousands of dollars in a wedding. After you have completed this budget, you will have a much better idea of what your wedding will cost. You can then prioritize and allocate your money accordingly.

This budget is divided into fifteen categories: Ceremony, Wedding Attire, Photography, Videography, Stationery, Reception, Music, Bakery, Flowers, Decorations, Transportation, Rental Items, Gifts, Parties, and Miscellaneous.

At the beginning of each category is the percentage of a total wedding budget that is typically spent in that category, based on national averages. Multiply your intended wedding budget by this percentage and write that amount in the "Typically" space provided.

To determine the total cost of your wedding, estimate the amount of money you will spend on each item in the budget analysis and write that amount in the "Budget" column after each item. Next to each expense item is the page number where you can find detailed information about it. Items printed in italics are traditionally paid for by the groom or his family.

Add all the "Budget" amounts within each category and write the total amount in the "Subtotal" space at the end of each category. Then add all the "Subtotal" figures to come up with your final wedding budget. The "Actual" column is for you to input your actual expenses as you purchase items or hire your service providers. Writing down the actual expenses will help you stay within your budget.

For example, if your total wedding budget is $60,000, write this amount at the top of page 28. To figure your typical ceremony expenses, multiply $60,000 by .05 (5%) to get $3,000. Write this amount on the "Typically" line in the "Ceremony" category to serve as a guide for all your ceremony expenses.

If you find, after adding up all your "Subtotals," that the total amount is more than what you had in mind to spend, simply decide which items are more important to you and adjust your expenses accordingly.

CHECKLIST OF BUDGET ITEMS

CEREMONY

- ❑ Ceremony Site Fee
- ❑ *Officiant's Fee*
- ❑ *Officiant's Gratuity*
- ❑ Guest Book/Pen/Penholder
- ❑ Ring Bearer Pillow
- ❑ Flower Girl Basket

WEDDING ATTIRE

- ❑ Bridal Gown
- ❑ Alterations
- ❑ Headpiece/Veil
- ❑ Gloves
- ❑ Jewelry
- ❑ Garter/Stockings
- ❑ Shoes
- ❑ Hairdresser
- ❑ Makeup Artist
- ❑ Manicure/Pedicure
- ❑ *Groom's Formal Wear*

PHOTOGRAPHY

- ❑ Bride & Groom's Album
- ❑ Engagement Photograph
- ❑ Formal Bridal Portrait
- ❑ Parents' Album
- ❑ Proofs/Previews
- ❑ Digital Files
- ❑ Extra Prints

VIDEOGRAPHY

- ❑ Main Video
- ❑ Titles
- ❑ Extra Hours
- ❑ Photo Montage
- ❑ Extra Copies

STATIONERY

- ❑ Invitations
- ❑ Response Cards
- ❑ Reception Cards
- ❑ Ceremony Cards
- ❑ Pew Cards
- ❑ Seating/Place Cards
- ❑ Rain Cards
- ❑ Maps
- ❑ Ceremony Programs
- ❑ Announcements
- ❑ Thank-You Notes
- ❑ Stamps
- ❑ Calligraphy
- ❑ Napkins/Matchbooks

RECEPTION

- ❑ Reception Site Fee
- ❑ Hors d'Oeuvres
- ❑ Main Meal/Caterer
- ❑ Liquor/Beverages
- ❑ Bartending/Bar Setup Fee
- ❑ Corkage Fee
- ❑ Fee to Pour Coffee

RECEPTION (CONT.)

- ❑ Service Providers' Meals
- ❑ Gratuity
- ❑ Party Favors
- ❑ Disposable Cameras
- ❑ Rose Petals/Rice
- ❑ Gift Attendant
- ❑ Parking Fee/Valet Services

MUSIC

- ❑ Ceremony Music
- ❑ Reception Music

BAKERY

- ❑ Wedding Cake
- ❑ *Groom's Cake*
- ❑ Cake Delivery/Setup Fee
- ❑ Cake-Cutting Fee
- ❑ Cake Top
- ❑ Cake Knife/Toasting Glasses

FLOWERS

BOUQUETS
- ❑ *Bride*
- ❑ Tossing
- ❑ Maid of Honor
- ❑ Bridesmaid

Items in italics are traditionally paid for by the groom or his family.

FLOWERS (CONT.)

FLORAL HAIRPIECES
- ❏ Maid of Honor/Bridesmaids
- ❏ Flower Girl

CORSAGES
- ❏ *Bride's Going Away*
- ❏ *Family Members*

BOUTONNIERES
- ❏ *Groom*
- ❏ *Ushers/Other Family Members*

CEREMONY SITE
- ❏ Main Altar
- ❏ Altar Candelabra
- ❏ Aisle Pews

RECEPTION SITE
- ❏ Head Table
- ❏ Guest Tables
- ❏ Buffet Table
- ❏ Punch Table
- ❏ Cake Table
- ❏ Cake
- ❏ Cake Knife
- ❏ Toasting Glasses
- ❏ Floral Delivery/Setup Fee

DECORATIONS
- ❏ Table Centerpieces
- ❏ Balloons

TRANSPORTATION
- ❏ Transportation

RENTAL ITEMS
- ❏ Bridal Slip
- ❏ Ceremony Accessories
- ❏ Tent/Canopy
- ❏ Dance Floor
- ❏ Tables/Chairs
- ❏ Linen/Tableware
- ❏ Heaters
- ❏ Lanterns
- ❏ Other Rental Items

GIFTS
- ❏ *Bride's Gift*
- ❏ Groom's Gift
- ❏ Bridesmaids' Gifts
- ❏ *Ushers' Gifts*

PARTIES
- ❏ Bridesmaids' Luncheon
- ❏ *Rehearsal Dinner*

MISCELLANEOUS
- ❏ Newspaper Announcements
- ❏ *Marriage License*
- ❏ *Prenuptial Agreement*
- ❏ Bridal Gown Preservation
- ❏ Bridal Bouquet Preservation
- ❏ Wedding Consultant
- ❏ Wedding Planning Online
- ❏ Taxes

Items in italics are traditionally paid for by the groom or his family.

BUDGET ANALYSIS

WEDDING BUDGET	Budget	Actual
YOUR TOTAL WEDDING BUDGET	$	$
CEREMONY (Typically = 5% of Budget)	$	$
pg. 35 Ceremony Site Fee	$	$
pg. 36 *Officiant's Fee*	$	$
pg. 36 *Officiant's Gratuity*	$	$
pg. 36 Guest Book/Pen/Penholder	$	$
pg. 37 Ring Bearer Pillow	$	$
pg. 37 Flower Girl Basket	$	$
SUBTOTAL 1	$	$

WEDDING ATTIRE	Budget	Actual
WEDDING ATTIRE (Typically = 10% of Budget)	$	$
pg. 49 Bridal Gown	$	$
pg. 51 Alterations	$	$
pg. 51 Headpiece/Veil	$	$
pg. 52 Gloves	$	$
pg. 52 Jewelry	$	$
pg. 52 Garter/Stockings	$	$
pg. 53 Shoes	$	$
pg. 53 Hairdresser	$	$
pg. 53 Makeup Artist	$	$
pg. 54 Manicure/Pedicure	$	$
pg. 54 *Groom's Formal Wear*	$	$
SUBTOTAL 2	$	$

PHOTOGRAPHY	Budget	Actual
PHOTOGRAPHY (Typically = 9% of Budget)	$	$
pg. 63 Bride & Groom's Album	$	$
pg. 65 Engagement Photograph	$	$
pg. 65 Formal Bridal Portrait	$	$
pg. 66 Parents' Album	$	$
pg. 66 Proofs/Previews	$	$

Items in italics are traditionally paid for by the groom or his family.

WEDDING BUDGET	Budget	Actual
PHOTOGRAPHY (CONT.)		
pg. 66 Digital Files	$	$
pg. 67 Extra Prints	$	$
SUBTOTAL 3	$	$

VIDEOGRAPHY (Typically = 5% of Budget)	Budget	Actual
VIDEOGRAPHY (Typically = 5% of Budget)	$	$
pg. 77 Main Video	$	$
pg. 79 Titles	$	$
pg. 79 Extra Hours	$	$
pg. 79 Photo Montage	$	$
pg. 80 Extra Copies	$	$
SUBTOTAL 4	$	$

STATIONERY	Budget	Actual
STATIONERY (Typically = 4% of Budget)	$	$
pg. 85 Invitations	$	$
pg. 90 Response Cards	$	$
pg. 91 Reception Cards	$	$
pg. 92 Ceremony Cards	$	$
pg. 92 Pew Cards	$	$
pg. 92 Seating/Place Cards	$	$
pg. 93 Rain Cards	$	$
pg. 93 Maps	$	$
pg. 93 Ceremony Programs	$	$
pg. 94 Announcements	$	$
pg. 94 Thank-You Notes	$	$
pg. 95 Stamps	$	$
pg. 95 Calligraphy	$	$
pg. 95 Napkins/Matchbooks	$	$
SUBTOTAL 5	$	$

Items in italics are traditionally paid for by the groom or his family.

BUDGET ANALYSIS (CONT.)

WEDDING BUDGET	Budget	Actual
RECEPTION (Typically = 35% of Budget)	$	$
pg. 109 Reception Site Fee	$	$
pg. 110 Hors d'Oeuvres	$	$
pg. 110 Main Meal/Caterer	$	$
pg. 112 Liquor/Beverages	$	$
pg. 113 Bartending/Bar Setup Fee	$	$
pg. 114 Corkage Fee	$	$
pg. 114 Fee to Pour Coffee	$	$
pg. 114 Service Providers' Meals	$	$
pg. 115 Gratuity	$	$
pg. 115 Party Favors	$	$
pg. 115 Disposable Cameras	$	$
pg. 116 Rose Petals/Rice	$	$
pg. 117 Gift Attendant	$	$
pg. 117 Parking Fee/Valet Services	$	$
SUBTOTAL 6	$	$
MUSIC (Typically = 5% of Budget)	$	$
pg. 131 Ceremony Music	$	$
pg. 132 Reception Music	$	$
SUBTOTAL 7	$	$
BAKERY (Typically = 2% of Budget)	$	$
pg. 139 Wedding Cake	$	$
pg. 140 *Groom's Cake*	$	$
pg. 140 Cake Delivery/Setup Fee	$	$
pg. 140 Cake-Cutting Fee	$	$
pg. 141 Cake Top	$	$
pg. 141 Cake Knife/Toasting Glasses	$	$
SUBTOTAL 8	$	$

Items in italics are traditionally paid for by the groom or his family.

WEDDING BUDGET	Budget	Actual
FLOWERS (Typically = 6% of Budget)	$	$
BOUQUETS	$	$
pg. 145 *Bride*	$	$
pg. 147 Tossing	$	$
pg. 147 Maid of Honor	$	$
pg. 147 Bridesmaids	$	$
FLORAL HAIRPIECES	$	$
pg. 148 Maid of Honor/Bridesmaids	$	$
pg. 148 Flower Girl	$	$
CORSAGES	$	$
pg. 148 *Bride's Going Away*	$	$
pg. 149 *Family Members*	$	$
BOUTONNIERES	$	$
pg. 149 *Groom*	$	$
pg. 150 Ushers/Other Family Members	$	$
CEREMONY SITE	$	$
pg. 150 Main Altar	$	$
pg. 151 Altar Candelabra	$	$
pg. 151 Aisle Pews	$	$
RECEPTION SITE	$	$
pg. 152 Reception Site	$	$
pg. 152 Head Table	$	$
pg. 152 Guest Tables	$	$
pg. 153 Buffet Table	$	$
pg. 153 Punch Table	$	$
pg. 153 Cake Table	$	$
pg. 154 Cake	$	$
pg. 154 Cake Knife	$	$
pg. 154 Toasting Glasses	$	$
pg. 154 Floral Delivery/Setup Fee	$	$
SUBTOTAL 9	$	$

Items in italics are traditionally paid for by the groom or his family.

WEDDING BUDGET	Budget	Actual
DECORATIONS (Typically = 3% of Budget	$	$
pg. 193 Table Centerpieces	$	$
pg. 194 Balloons	$	$
SUBTOTAL 10	$	$

	Budget	Actual
TRANSPORTATION (Typically = 2% of Budget)	$	$
pg. 195 Transportation	$	$
SUBTOTAL 11	$	$

	Budget	Actual
RENTAL ITEMS (Typically = 3% of Budget)	$	$
pg. 199 Bridal Slip	$	$
pg. 199 Ceremony Accessories	$	$
pg. 200 Tent/Canopy	$	$
pg. 201 Dance Floor	$	$
pg. 201 Tables/Chairs	$	$
pg. 201 Linen/Tableware	$	$
pg. 202 Heaters	$	$
pg. 202 Lanterns	$	$
pg. 202 Other Rental Items	$	$
SUBTOTAL 12	$	$

	Budget	Actual
GIFTS (Typically = 3% of Budget)	$	$
pg. 209 *Bride's Gift*	$	$
pg. 209 Groom's Gift	$	$
pg. 210 Bridesmaids' Gifts	$	$
pg. 210 *Ushers' Gifts*	$	$
SUBTOTAL 13	$	$

Items in italics are traditionally paid for by the groom or his family.

WEDDING BUDGET	Budget	Actual
PARTIES (Typically = 4% of Budget)	$	$
pg. 212 Bridesmaids' Luncheon	$	$
pg. 212 *Rehearsal Dinner*	$	$
SUBTOTAL 14	$	$

MISCELLANEOUS	Budget	Actual
MISCELLANEOUS (Typically = 4% of Budget)	$	$
pg. 213 Newspaper Announcements	$	$
pg. 214 *Marriage License*	$	$
pg. 214 *Prenuptial Agreement*	$	$
pg. 215 Bridal Gown Preservation	$	$
pg. 215 Bridal Bouquet Preservation	$	$
pg. 216 Wedding Consultant	$	$
pg. 217 Wedding Planning Online	$	$
pg. 217 Taxes	$	$
SUBTOTAL 15	$	$

	Budget	Actual
GRAND TOTAL (Add "Budget" & "Actual" Subtotals 1-15)	$	$

Items in italics are traditionally paid for by the groom or his family.

VENDOR PAYMENT TRACKING CHART

VENDOR	Business Name & Phone Number	Website & E-mail Address	Contract Date & Total Cost	Deposit & Date	Next Pmt. & Date	Final Pmt. & Date
Wedding Consultant						
Ceremony Site						
Officiant						
Reception Site						
Caterer						
Liquor Services						
Wedding Gown						
Tuxedo Rental						
Photographer						
Videographer						
Stationer						
Calligrapher						
Music: Ceremony						
Music: Reception						
Florist						
Bakery						
Decorations						
Ice Sculpture						
Party Favors						
Balloonist						
Transportation						
Rental & Supplies						
Gift Suppliers						
Valet Services						
Gift Attendant						
Rehearsal Dinner						

"In dreams and in love there
are no impossibilities."
~ Janos Arany

CEREMONY SITE FEE 35

OFFICIANT'S FEE 36

OFFICIANT'S GRATUITY 36

GUEST BOOK/PEN/PENHOLDER 36

RING BEARER PILLOW 37

FLOWER GIRL BASKET 37

CEREMONY SITE COMPARISON CHART 38

CEREMONY READING SELECTIONS 42

CEREMONY MUSIC SELECTIONS 43

PERSONALIZED VOWS 44

PEW SEATING ARRANGEMENTS 45

UNIQUE WEDDING IDEAS 47

    IDEAS TO PERSONALIZE YOUR CEREMONY 47

    IDEAS TO PERSONALIZE YOUR MARRIAGE VOWS 48

CEREMONY

PHOTO: KAREN FRENCH

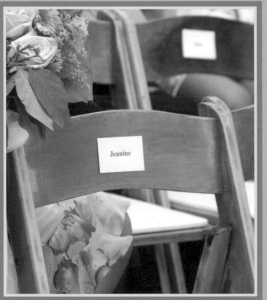

CEREMONY

YOUR CEREMONY IS A REFLECTION OF WHO YOU ARE. It can be as simple or as elaborate as you desire. Many people choose to have a traditional ceremony in a church, while others have taken their special day outdoors to a park or the beach. These days, anything goes!

CEREMONY SITE FEE

The ceremony site fee is the fee to rent a facility for your wedding. In churches, cathedrals, chapels, temples, or synagogues, this fee may include the organist, wedding coordinator, custodian, changing rooms for the bridal party, and miscellaneous items such as kneeling cushions, aisle runner, and candelabra. Be sure to ask what the site fee includes prior to booking a facility. Throughout this book, the word church will be used to refer to the site where the ceremony will take place.

Options: Churches, cathedrals, chapels, temples, synagogues, private homes, gardens, hotels, clubs, halls, parks, museums, yachts, wineries, beaches, and hot air balloons.

Things to Consider: Your selection of a ceremony site will be influenced by the formality of your wedding, the season of the year, the number of guests expected and your religious affiliation. Make sure you ask about restrictions or guidelines

regarding photography, videography, music, decorations, candles, and rice or rose petal-tossing. Consider issues such as proximity of the ceremony site to the reception site, parking availability, handicapped accessibility, and time constraints.

Tips to Save Money: Have your ceremony at the same facility as your reception to save a second rental fee. Set a realistic guest list and stick to it. Hire an experienced wedding consultant. At a church or temple, ask if there is another wedding that day and share the cost of floral decorations with that bride. Membership in a church, temple, or club can reduce rental fees. At a garden wedding, have guests stand and omit the cost of renting chairs.

Price Range: $100 - $1,000

CEREMONY

OFFICIANT'S FEE

The officiant's fee is the fee paid to the person who performs your wedding ceremony.

Options: Priest, Clergyman, Minister, Pastor, Chaplain, Rabbi, Judge, or Justice of the Peace. Discuss with your officiant the readings you would like incorporated into your ceremony. Some popular readings are:

Beatitudes	Corinthians 13:1-13	Ecclesiastes 3:1-9
Ephesians 3:14-19; 5:1-2	Genesis 1:26-28	Genesis 2:4-9, 15-24
Hosea 2:19-21	Isaiah 61:10I	John 4:7-16
John 15:9-12, 17:22-24	Mark 10:6-9	Proverbs 31:10-31
Romans 12:1-2, 9-18	Ruth 1:16-17	Tobit 8:56-58

Things to Consider: Some officiants may not accept a fee, depending on your relationship with him/her. If a fee is refused, send a donation to the officiant's church or synagogue.

Price Range: $100 - $500

OFFICIANT'S GRATUITY

The officiant's gratuity is a discretionary amount of money given to the officiant.

Things to Consider: This amount should depend on your relationship with the officiant and the amount of time s/he has spent with you prior to the ceremony. The groom puts this fee in a sealed envelope and gives it to his best man or wedding consultant, who gives it to the officiant either before or immediately after the ceremony.

Price Range: $50 - $250

GUEST BOOK/PEN/PENHOLDER

The guest book is a formal register that your guests sign as they arrive at the ceremony or reception. It serves as a memento of who attended your wedding. This book is often placed outside the ceremony or reception site, along with an elegant pen and penholder. A guest book attendant is responsible for inviting all guests to sign in. A younger sibling or close friend who is not part of the wedding party may be well-suited for this position.

Options: There are many styles of guest books, pens, and penholders to choose from. Some books have space for your guests to write a short note to the bride and groom.

Things to Consider: Make sure you have more than one pen in case one runs out of ink. If you are planning a large ceremony (over 300 guests), consider having more than one book and pen so that your guests don't have to wait in line to sign in.

Price Range: $30 - $100

RING BEARER PILLOW

The ring bearer, usually a boy between the ages of four and eight, carries the bride and groom's rings or mock rings on a pillow. He follows the maid of honor and precedes the flower girl or bride in the processional.

Options: These pillows come in many styles and colors. You can find them at most gift shops and bridal boutiques.

Things to Consider: If the ring bearer is very young (less than 7 years), place mock rings on the pillow in place of the real rings to prevent losing them. If mock rings are used, instruct your ring bearer to put the pillow upside down during the recessional so your guests don't see them.

Tips to Save Money: Make your own ring bearer pillow by taking a small white pillow and attaching a pretty ribbon to it to hold the rings.

Price Range: $15 - $75

FLOWER GIRL BASKET

The flower girl, usually between the ages of four and eight, carries a basket filled with flowers, rose petals, or paper rose petals to scatter as she walks down the aisle. She follows the ring bearer or maid of honor and precedes the bride during the processional.

Options: Flower girl baskets come in many styles and colors. You can find them at most florists, gift shops, and bridal boutiques.

Things to Consider: Discuss any restrictions regarding rose petal, flower, or paper-tossing with your ceremony site. Select a basket which complements your guest book and ring bearer pillow. If the flower girl is very young (less than 7 years), consider giving her a small bouquet instead of a flower basket.

Tips to Save Money: Ask your florist if you can borrow a basket and attach a pretty white bow to it.

Price Range: $20 - $75

CEREMONY SITE COMPARISON CHART

QUESTIONS	POSSIBILITY 1	POSSIBILITY 2
What is the name of the ceremony site?		
What is the website and e-mail of the ceremony site?		
What is the address of the ceremony site?		
What is the name and phone number of my contact person?		
What dates and times are available?		
Do vows need to be approved?		
What is the ceremony site fee?		
What is the payment policy?		
What is the cancellation policy?		
Does the facility have liability insurance?		
What are the minimum/maximum number of guests allowed?		
What is the denomination, if any, of the facility?		
What restrictions are there with regards to religion?		
Is an officiant available? At what cost?		
Are outside officiants allowed?		
Are any musical instruments available for our use?		
If so, what is the fee?		

POSSIBILITY 3	POSSIBILITY 4	POSSIBILITY 5	POSSIBILITY 6

CEREMONY SITE COMPARISON CHART (CONT.)

QUESTIONS	POSSIBILITY 1	POSSIBILITY 2
What music restrictions are there, if any?		
What photography restrictions are there, if any?		
What videography restrictions are there, if any?		
Are there any restrictions for rice/petal-tossing?		
Are candlelight ceremonies allowed?		
What floral decorations are available/allowed?		
When is my rehearsal to be scheduled?		
Is there handicap accessibility and parking?		
How many parking spaces are available for my wedding party?		
Where are they located?		
How many parking spaces are available for my guests?		
What rental items are necessary?		
What is the fee?		

POSSIBILITY 3	POSSIBILITY 4	POSSIBILITY 5	POSSIBILITY 6

CEREMONY READING SELECTIONS

SOURCE	Selection	Read By	When

WHEN	Selection	Composer	Played By
Prelude 1			
Prelude 2			
Prelude 3			
Processional			
Bride's Processional			
Ceremony 1			
Ceremony 2			
Ceremony 3			
Recessional			
Postlude			
Other:			
Other:			
Other:			
Other:			
Other:			
Other:			
Other:			

PERSONALIZED VOWS

BRIDE'S VOWS:

_____

_____

_____

_____

_____

_____

_____

GROOM'S VOWS:

_____

_____

_____

_____

_____

_____

_____

_____

PERSONALIZED RING CEREMONY:

_____

_____

_____

_____

_____

_____

_____

PEW SEATING ARRANGEMENTS

Complete this form only after finalizing your guest list.

BRIDE'S FAMILY SECTION

• PEW __

_____
_____
_____
_____
_____
_____
_____
_____
_____

• PEW __

_____
_____
_____
_____
_____
_____
_____
_____
_____

• PEW __

_____
_____
_____
_____
_____
_____
_____
_____
_____

• PEW __

_____
_____
_____
_____
_____
_____
_____
_____
_____

• PEW __

_____
_____
_____
_____
_____
_____
_____
_____
_____

• PEW __

_____
_____
_____
_____
_____
_____
_____
_____
_____

• PEW __

_____
_____
_____
_____
_____
_____
_____
_____

• PEW __

_____
_____
_____
_____
_____
_____
_____
_____

• PEW __

_____
_____
_____
_____
_____
_____
_____
_____

PEW SEATING ARRANGEMENTS (CONT.)

Complete this form only after finalizing your guest list.

GROOM'S FAMILY SECTION

• **PEW __**
_____
_____
_____
_____
_____
_____
_____
_____

• **PEW __**
_____
_____
_____
_____
_____
_____
_____
_____

• **PEW __**
_____
_____
_____
_____
_____
_____
_____
_____

• **PEW __**
_____
_____
_____
_____
_____
_____
_____
_____

• **PEW __**
_____
_____
_____
_____
_____
_____
_____
_____

• **PEW __**
_____
_____
_____
_____
_____
_____
_____
_____

• **PEW __**
_____
_____
_____
_____
_____
_____
_____
_____

• **PEW __**
_____
_____
_____
_____
_____
_____
_____
_____

• **PEW __**
_____
_____
_____
_____
_____
_____
_____
_____

UNIQUE WEDDING IDEAS

IDEAS TO PERSONALIZE YOUR CEREMONY

Regardless of your religious affiliation, there are numerous ways in which you can personalize your wedding ceremony to add a more creative touch. If you're planning a religious ceremony at a church or temple, be sure to discuss all ideas with your officiant.

The following list incorporates some ideas to personalize your wedding ceremony.

- Invite the bride's mother to be part of the processional. Have her walk down the aisle with you and your father. (This is the traditional Jewish processional.)

- Invite the groom's parents to be part of the processional as well.

- Ask friends and family members to perform special readings.

- Ask a friend or family member with musical talent to perform at the ceremony.

- Incorporate poetry and/or literature into your readings.

- Change places with the officiant and face your guests during the ceremony.

- Light a unity candle to symbolize your two lives joining together as one.

- Drink wine from a shared "loving" cup to symbolize bonding with each other.

- Hand a rose to each of your mothers as you pass by them during the recessional.

- Release white doves into the air after being pronounced "husband and wife."

- If the ceremony is held outside on a grassy area, have your guests toss grass or flower seeds over you instead of rice.

- Publicly express gratitude for all that your parents have done for you.

- Use a canopy to designate an altar for a non-church setting. Decorate it in ways that are symbolic or meaningful to you.

- Burn incense to give the ceremony an exotic feeling.

UNIQUE WEDDING IDEAS

IDEAS TO PERSONALIZE YOUR MARRIAGE VOWS

Regardless of your religious affiliation and whether you're planning a church or outdoor ceremony, there are ways in which you can personalize your marriage vows to make them more meaningful for you. As with all your ceremony plans, be sure to discuss your ideas for marriage vows with your officiant.

The following are some ideas that you might want to consider when planning your marriage vows:

- You and your fiancé could write your own personal marriage vows and keep them secret from one another until the actual ceremony.

- Incorporate your guests and family members into your vows by acknowledging their presence at the ceremony.

- Describe what you cherish most about your partner and what you hope for your future together.

- Describe your commitment to and love for one another.

- Discuss your feelings and beliefs about marriage.

- If either of you has children from a previous marriage, mention these children in your vows and discuss your mutual love for and commitment to them.

"Love is a great beautifier."
~ Louisa May Alcott

BRIDAL GOWN 49

ALTERATIONS 51

HEADPIECE/VEIL 51

GLOVES 52

JEWELRY.. 52

GARTER/STOCKINGS 52

SHOES... 53

HAIRDRESSER 53

MAKEUP ARTIST... 53

MANICURE/PEDICURE... 54

GROOM'S FORMAL WEAR 54

BRIDAL ATTIRE CHECKLIST 57

BRIDAL BOUTIQUE COMPARISON CHART.................. 58

BRIDAL ATTIRE INFORMATION SHEET 60

BRIDESMAIDS' ATTIRE.. 61

GROOMSMEN'S ATTIRE.. 62

ATTIRE

ATTIRE

BRIDAL GOWNS COME IN A WIDE VARIETY OF STYLES, materials, colors, lengths, and prices. You should order your gown at least four to six months before your wedding if your gown has to be ordered and then fitted. In selecting your gown, keep in mind the time of year and formality of your wedding. It is a good idea to look at bridal magazines to compare the various styles and colors. If you see a gown you like, call boutiques in your area to see if they carry that line. Always try on a gown before ordering it.

BRIDAL GOWN

Options: Different gown styles complement different body types. Here are some tips when choosing your dress:

• **A short, heavy figure:** To look taller and slimmer, avoid knit fabrics. Use the princess or A-line style. Chiffon is the best fabric choice because it produces a floating effect and camouflages weight.

• **A short, thin figure:** A shirtwaist or natural waist style with bouffant skirt will produce a taller, more rounded figure. Chiffon, velvet, lace, and Schiffli net are probably the best fabric choices.

• **A tall, heavy figure:** Princess or A-line styles are best for slimming the figure; satin, chiffon, and lace fabrics are recommended.

• **A tall, thin figure:** Tiers or flounces will help reduce the impression of height. A shirtwaist or natural waist style with a full skirt are ideal choices. Satin and lace are the best fabrics.

The guidelines below will help you select the most appropriate gown for your wedding:

Informal wedding:
>   Street-length gown or suit
>   Corsage or small bouquet
>   No veil or train

Semiformal wedding:
>   Floor-length gown
>   Chapel train
>   Fingertip veil
>   Small bouquet

ATTIRE

Formal daytime wedding:	Floor-length gown
	Chapel or sweep train
	Fingertip veil or hat
	Gloves
	Medium-sized bouquet
Formal evening wedding:	Same as formal daytime except longer veil
Very formal wedding:	Floor-length gown
	Cathedral train
	Full-length veil
	Elaborate headpiece
	Long sleeves or long arm-covering gloves
	Cascading bouquet

Things to Consider: In selecting your bridal gown, keep in mind the time of year and formality of your wedding. It is a good idea to look at bridal magazines to compare the various styles and colors. If you see a gown you like, call boutiques in your area to see if they carry that line. Always try on the gown before ordering it.

When ordering a gown, make sure you order the correct size. If you are between sizes, order the larger one. You can always have your gown tailored down to fit, but it is not always possible to have it enlarged or to lose enough weight to fit into it! Don't forget to ask when your gown will arrive, and be sure to get this in writing. The gown should arrive at least six weeks before the wedding so you can have it tailored and select the appropriate accessories to complement it.

It's a good idea to put on "evening" makeup before going to try on dresses—trying on your wedding gown with a plain face is like trying on an evening dress wearing sneakers!

Beware: Some gown manufacturers suggest ordering a size larger than needed. This requires more alterations, which may mean extra charges. It is a good idea to locate a few tailors in your area and ask for alteration pricing in advance. Many boutiques offer tailoring services, but you will often find a better price by finding an independent tailor specializing in bridal gown alterations. Also, gowns often fail to arrive on time, creating unnecessary stress for you. Be sure to order your gown with enough time to allow for delivery delays and also be sure to check the reputation of the boutique before buying.

Tips to Save Money: Consider renting a gown or buying one secondhand. Renting a gown usually costs about 40 to 60 percent of its retail price. Consider this practical option if you are not planning to preserve the gown. The disadvantage of renting, however, is that your options are more limited. Also, a rented gown usually does not fit as well as a custom tailored gown.

ATTIRE

Ask about discontinued styles and gowns. Watch for clearances and sales, or buy your gown "off the rack." Restore or refurbish a family heirloom gown. If you have a friend, sister, or other family member who is planning a wedding, consider purchasing a gown that you could both wear. Change the veil and headpiece to personalize it.

Price Range: $500 - $10,000

ALTERATIONS

Alterations may be necessary to make your gown fit perfectly and conform smoothly to your body.

Things to Consider: Alterations usually require several fittings. Allow four to six weeks for alterations to be completed. However, do not alter your gown months before the wedding. Your weight may fluctuate during the final weeks of planning, and the gown might not fit properly. Alterations are usually not included in the cost of the gown.

You may also want to consider making some modifications to your gown such as shortening or lengthening the train, customizing the sleeves, beading and so forth. Ask your bridal boutique what they charge for the modifications you are considering.

Tips to Save Money: Consider hiring an independent tailor. Their fees are usually lower than bridal boutiques.

Price Range: $75 - $500

HEADPIECE/VEIL

The headpiece is the part of the bride's outfit to which the veil is attached.

Options for Headpieces: Bow, Garden Hat, Headband, Juliet Cap, Mantilla, Pillbox, Pouf, Snood, Tiara.

Options for Veils: Ballet, Bird Cage, Blusher, Cathedral Length, Chapel Length, Fingertip, Flyaway.

Things to Consider: The headpiece should complement but not overshadow your gown. In addition to the headpiece, you might want a veil. Veils come in different styles and lengths.

Select a length which complements the length of your train. Consider the total look you're trying to achieve with your gown, headpiece, veil, and hairstyle. If possible, schedule your hair "test appointment" the day you go veil shopping—you'll be able to see how your veil looks on your hairdo!

ATTIRE

Tips to Save Money: Some boutiques offer a free headpiece or veil with the purchase of a gown. Make sure you ask for this before purchasing your gown.

Price Range: $60 - $500

GLOVES

Gloves add a nice touch to either short-sleeved, three-quarter length, or sleeveless gowns.

Options: Gloves come in various styles and lengths. Depending on the length of your sleeves, select gloves that reach above your elbow, just below your elbow, halfway between your wrist and elbow, or only to your wrist.

Things to Consider: You may want to consider finger less mitts, which allow the groom to place the wedding ring on your ring finger without having to remove your glove. You should not wear gloves if your gown has long sleeves, or if you're planning a small, at-home wedding.

Price Range: $15 - $100

JEWELRY

Jewelry can beautifully accent your dress and be the perfect finishing touch.

Options: Select pieces of jewelry that can be classified as "something old, something new, something borrowed, or something blue."

Things to Consider: Brides look best with just a few pieces of jewelry—perhaps a string of pearls and earrings with a simple bracelet. Purchase complementary jewelry for your bridesmaids, to match the colors of their dresses. This will give your bridal party a coordinated look.

Price Range: $60 - $2,000

GARTER/STOCKINGS

It is customary for the bride to wear a garter just above the knee on her wedding day. After the bouquet tossing ceremony, the groom takes the garter off the bride's leg. All the single men gather on the dance floor. The groom then tosses the garter to them over his back. According to age-old tradition, whoever catches the garter is the next to be married!

Stockings should be selected with care, especially if the groom will be removing a garter from your leg at the reception. Consider having your maid of honor carry an extra pair, just in case you get a run.

Things to Consider: You will need to choose the proper music for this event. A popular and fun song to play during the garter removal ceremony is *The Stripper*, by David Rose.

Price Range: $15 - $60

SHOES

Things to Consider: Make sure you select comfortable shoes that complement your gown. Don't forget to break them in well before your wedding day. Tight shoes can make you miserable and ruin your otherwise perfect day!

Price Range: $50 - $500

HAIRDRESSER

Many brides prefer to have their hair professionally arranged with their headpiece the day of the wedding rather than trying to do it themselves.

Things to Consider: Have your professional hairdresser experiment with your hair and headpiece before your wedding day so there are no surprises. Most hairdressers will include the cost of a sample session in your package. They will try several styles on you and write down the specifics of each one so that things go quickly and smoothly on your wedding day. On the big day, you can go to the salon or have the stylist meet you at your home or dressing site. Consider having him/her arrange your bridal party's hair for a consistent look.

Tips to Save Money: Negotiate having your hair arranged free of charge or at a discount in exchange for bringing your mother, your fiancé's mother, and your bridal party to the salon.

Price Range: $50 - $200 per person

MAKEUP ARTIST

A professional makeup artist will apply makeup that should last throughout the day and will often provide you with samples for touch-ups.

ATTIRE

Things to Consider: It's smart to go for a trial run before the day of the wedding so there are no surprises. You can either go to the salon or have the makeup artist meet you at your home or dressing site. Consider having him/her apply makeup for your mother, your fiancé's mother, and your bridesmaids for a consistent look. In selecting a makeup artist, make sure s/he has been trained in makeup for photography. It is very important to wear the proper amount of makeup for photographs.

Consider having your makeup trial right before your hairdresser trial—that way you'll see how your hair looks with your makeup on. It can make a big difference.

Tips to Save Money: Try to negotiate having your makeup applied free of charge or at a discount in exchange for bringing your mother, your fiancé's mother, and your wedding party to the salon.

Price Range: $30 - $150 per person

MANICURE/PEDICURE

As a final touch, it's nice to have a professional manicure and/or pedicure the day of your wedding.

Things to Consider: Don't forget to bring the appropriate color nail polish with you for your appointment. You can either go to the salon or have the manicurist meet you at your home or dressing site. Consider having him/her give your mother, your fiancé's mother, and your bridesmaids a manicure in the same color.

Tips to Save Money: Try to negotiate getting a manicure or pedicure free of charge or at a discount in exchange for bringing your mother, your fiancé's mother, and your wedding party to the salon.

Price Range: $15 - $75 per person

GROOM'S FORMAL WEAR

The groom should select his formal wear based on the formality of the wedding. For a semiformal or formal wedding, the groom will need a tuxedo. A tuxedo is the formal jacket worn by men on special or formal occasions. The most popular colors are black, white, and gray.

Options: Use the following guidelines to select customary attire for the groom:

Informal wedding: Business suit
                                White dress shirt and tie

Semiformal daytime:	Formal suit
	White dress shirt
	Cummerbund or vest
	Four-in-hand or bow tie
Semiformal evening:	Formal suit or dinner jacket
	Matching trousers
	White shirt
	Cummerbund or vest
	Black bow tie
	Cuff links and studs
Formal daytime:	Cutaway or stroller jacket
	Waistcoat
	Striped trousers
	White wing-collared shirt
	Striped tie
	Studs and cuff links
Formal evening:	Black dinner jacket
	Matching trousers
	Waistcoat
	White tuxedo shirt
	Bow tie
	Cummerbund or vest
	Cuff links
Very formal daytime:	Cutaway coat
	Wing-collared shirt
	Ascot
	Striped trousers
	Cuff links
	Gloves
Very formal evening:	Black tailcoat
	Matching striped trousers
	Bow tie
	White wing-collared shirt
	Waistcoat
	Patent leather shoes
	Studs and cuff links
	Gloves

ATTIRE

Things to Consider: In selecting your formal wear, keep in mind the formality of your wedding, the time of day, and the bride's gown. Consider darker colors for a fall or winter wedding and lighter colors for a spring or summer wedding. When selecting a place to rent your tuxedo, check the reputation of the shop. Make sure they have a wide variety of makes and styles to choose from.

Reserve tuxedos for yourself and your ushers several weeks before the wedding to insure a wide selection and to allow enough time for alterations. Plan to pick up the tuxedos a few days before the wedding to allow time for last-minute alterations in case they don't fit properly. Out-of-town men in your wedding party can be sized at any tuxedo shop. They can send their measurements to you or directly to the shop where you are going to rent your tuxedos.

Ask about the store's return policy and be sure you delegate to the appropriate person (usually your best man) the responsibility of returning all tuxedos within the time allotted. Ushers customarily pay for their own tuxedos.

Tips to Save Money: Try to negotiate getting your tuxedo for free or at a discount in exchange for having your father, your fiancé's father, and ushers rent their tuxedos at that shop.

Price Range: $60 - $200

ITEM	Description	Source
Full Slip		
Garter		
Gloves		
Gown		
Handbag		
Jewelry		
Lingerie		
Panty Hose		
Petticoat or Slip		
Shoes		
Something Old		
Something New		
Something Borrowed		
Something Blue		
Stocking		
Veil/Hat		
Other:		
Other:		
Other:		
Other:		

BRIDAL BOUTIQUE COMPARISON CHART

QUESTIONS	POSSIBILITY 1	POSSIBILITY 2
What is the name of the bridal boutique?		
What is the website and e-mail of the bridal boutique?		
What is the address of the bridal boutique?		
What is the name and phone number of my contact person?		
What are your hours of operation? Are appointments needed?		
Do you offer any discounts or giveaways?		
What major bridal gown lines do you carry?		
Do you carry outfits for the mother of the bride?		
Do you carry bridesmaids gowns and/or tuxedos?		
Do you carry outfits for the flower girl and ring bearer?		
What is the cost of the desired bridal gown?		
What is the cost of the desired headpiece?		
Do you offer in-house alterations? If so, what are your fees?		
Do you carry bridal shoes? What is their price range?		
Do you dye shoes to match outfits?		
Do you rent bridal slips? If so, what is the rental fee?		
What is the estimated date of delivery for my gown?		
What is your payment policy/cancellation policy?		

POSSIBILITY 3	POSSIBILITY 4	POSSIBILITY 5	POSSIBILITY 6

BRIDAL ATTIRE INFORMATION SHEET

BRIDAL ATTIRE

Bridal Boutique:

Date Ordered:

Salesperson: Phone Number:

Address:

City: State: Zip Code:

Website:

E-mail:

Description of Dress:

	Manufacturer	Style	Size	Cost
Wedding Gown				
Headpiece				
Veil/Hat				
Shoes				

GOWN ALTERATIONS

Location:

Cost:

Tailor: Phone Number:

Address:

City: State: Zip Code:

Website:

E-mail:

	Manufacturer	Style
First Alteration		
Second Alteration		
Third Alteration		
Final Alteration		

BRIDESMAIDS' ATTIRE INFORMATION SHEET

Make as many copies of this form as needed.

BRIDESMAIDS' ATTIRE

Bridal Boutique: _____

Date Ordered: _____

Salesperson: _____ Phone Number: _____

Address: _____

City: _____ State: _____ Zip Code: _____

Website: _____

E-mail: _____

Description of Dress: _____

Cost: _____

Manufacturer: _____

Date Ready: _____

BRIDESMAIDS' SIZES

Name	Dress	Head	Weight	Height	Waist	Gloves	Shoes	Hose

GROOM/GROOMSMEN'S ATTIRE INFORMATION SHEET

Make as many copies of this form as needed.

GROOM/GROOMSMEN'S ATTIRE

Store Name:

Date Ordered:

Salesperson: Phone Number:

Address:

City: State: Zip Code:

Website:

E-mail:

Description of Tuxedo:

Cost:

Manufacturer:

Date Ready:

GROOM/GROOMSMEN'S SIZES   BRIDESMAIDS' SIZES

Name	Height	Weight	Waist	Sleeve	Inseam	Jacket	Neck	Shoes

"Love is a moment that lasts forever."
~ Anonymous

BRIDE & GROOM'S ALBUM..63

ENGAGEMENT PHOTOGRAPH 65

FORMAL BRIDAL PORTRAIT 65

PARENTS' ALBUM 66

PROOFS/PREVIEWS 66

DIGITAL FILES 66

EXTRA PRINTS...67

PHOTOGRAPHERS COMPARISON CHART.....................68

PHOTOGRAPHER'S INFORMATION..............................72

WEDDING PHOTOGRAPHS 74

   PRE-CEREMONY PHOTOGRAPHS...........................74

   CEREMONY PHOTOGRAPHS 75

   POST-CEREMONY PHOTOGRAPHS........................75

   RECEPTION PHOTOGRAPHS.................................76

PHOTOGRAPHY

PHOTO: KAREN FRENCH

PHOTOGRAPHY

THE PHOTOGRAPHS TAKEN AT YOUR WEDDING are the best way to preserve your special day. Chances are you and your fiancé will look at the photos many times during your lifetime. Therefore, hiring a good photographer is one of the most important tasks in planning your wedding.

BRIDE & GROOM'S ALBUM

The bride and groom's photo album is the traditional way to preserve your special day. You and your spouse will look at the photos many times during your lifetime. Therefore, hiring a good photographer is one of the most important tasks in planning your wedding.

Options: There are a large variety of wedding albums. They vary in size, color, material, construction and price. Traditional-style albums frame each individual photo in a mat on the page. Digitally designed "Montage" albums group the photos in a creatively designed fashion for a more modern look.

Find one that you like and will feel proud of showing to your friends and family. Some of the most popular manufacturers of wedding albums are Art Leather, Leather Craftsman, Capri and Renaissance.

Keep in mind however, that the quality of the original photographs will determine how the finished album looks so choose your photographer for their skills, not necessarily the manufacturer of the album. Make sure you are shown the different styles of album available.

Different papers are available to print your photos, pearl and metallic as well as black and white can be chosen. Ask to see samples.

Things to Consider: Make sure you hire a photographer who specializes in weddings. Your photographer should be experienced in wedding procedures and familiar with your ceremony and reception sites. This will allow him/her to anticipate your next move and be in the proper place at the right time to capture all the special moments. Personal rapport is extremely important. The photographer may be an expert, but if you don't feel comfortable or at ease with him or her, your photography will reflect this. Comfort and compatibility with your photographer can make or break your wedding day and your photographs!

Look at his/her work. See if the

PHOTOGRAPHY

photographer captured the excitement and emotion of the bridal couple. Also, remember that the wedding album should unfold like a story book -- the story of your wedding. Be sure to discuss with your photographer the photos you want so that there is no misunderstanding. A good wedding photographer will plan the day with you to ensure that all the important moments are covered. It is acceptable to take a list of important photos to your planning session before the wedding (even one copied from a wedding planning book). This will keep you on track and ensure that you've asked about all the photos that are "must haves."

Ask to look at albums that the photographer has ready to be delivered, or proofs of weddings recently photographed. Study the photographer's style. It's fine if they tell you that they're skilled in "photojournalistic" or "candid" photography but, if that's so, you should see plenty of candid-style shots in their portfolio! Some photographers are known for formal poses, while others specialize in more candid, creative shots. Some can do both.

When asked to provide references, photographers will obviously give you names of clients that they know are pleased with their work. (Why give a name of someone who wasn't?) So keep this in mind if you decide to call a former client.

When comparing prices, compare the quantity and size of the photographs in your album and the type of album that each photographer will use. Ask how many photos will be taken on average at a wedding of your size. Some photographers do not work with proofs. Rather, they simply supply you with a finished album after the wedding. Doing this may reduce the cost of your album but will also reduce your selection of photographs. Many photographers will put your proofs on a DVD for viewing. This is much less bulky and an easy way to preview all of your wedding photos.

Beware: Make sure the photographer you interview is the specific person that will photograph your wedding. Many companies have more than one photographer. The more professional companies will make sure that you meet with (and view the work of) THE photographer that will photograph your wedding. This way you can get an idea of his/her style and personality and begin to establish a rapport with YOUR photographer. Your chosen photographers name should go on your contract!

Also, some churches do not allow photographs to be shot during the ceremony. Please find out the rules and present them to your photographer so he is knowledgeable about your site.

Tips to Save Money: Consider hiring a professional photographer for the formal shots of your ceremony only. You can then place disposable cameras on each table at the reception and let your guests take candid shots. This will save you a considerable amount of money in photography.

You can also lower the price of your album by paying for the photographs and then putting them into the album yourself. This is a very time-consuming task, so your photographer may reduce the price of his/her package if you opt to do this. To really save money, select a photographer who charges a flat fee to shoot the wedding and allows you to purchase the film.

Compare at least three photographers for quality, value, and price. Photographers who shoot weddings "on the side" are usually less expensive, but the quality of their photographs may not be as good. Select less 8 x 10s for your album and more 4 x 6s, and choose a moderately priced album. Ask for specials and package deals.

Price Range: $900 - $9,000

ENGAGEMENT PHOTOGRAPH

The engagement photograph can be sent to your local newspapers, along with information announcing your engagement to the public. This announcement is usually made by the bride's parents or her immediate family. More small-town papers do this currently. The larger city papers have mostly ceased to publish engagement announcements.

Things to Consider: The photograph (usually in black and white) was traditionally of the bride alone, but today is usually of the engaged couple. The engagement portrait(s) can also be used to create a guestbook full of photos with room for guests to sign or can be framed with a wide mat to sign.

Tips to Save Money: Look at engagement photographs in your local newspaper. Then have a friend or family member take a photo of you and your fiancé in a pose and with a backdrop similar to the ones you have seen.

Price Range: $75 - $300

FORMAL BRIDAL PORTRAIT

Only a few newspapers still accept a photograph of the Bride for insertion in the newspaper the day after your wedding. For the ones that do, you'll need a studio Bridal portrait done a few weeks before the wedding so the photo can be ready. This photo, along with the announcement should be sent to the paper well ahead of time.

Things to Consider: Some fine bridal salons provide an attractive background where the bride may arrange to have her formal bridal photograph taken after the final fitting of her gown. This will save you the hassle of bringing your gown and headpiece to the photographer's studio and dressing up once again.

Tips to Save Money: If you don't mind announcing your marriage several weeks after the wedding, consider having your formal portrait taken the day of your wedding. This will save you the studio costs and the hassle of getting dressed for the photo. The photograph will be more natural since the bridal bouquet will be the one you carry down the aisle. Also, brides are always most beautiful on their wedding day!

Price Range: $75 - $300

PHOTOGRAPHY

PARENTS' ALBUM

The parents' album is a smaller version of the bride and groom's album. It usually contains about twenty 5" x 7" photographs. Photos should be carefully selected for each individual family. If given as a gift, the album can be personalized with the bride and groom's names and date of their wedding on the front cover. Small "Coffee Table" books can also be created from digital files that are montaged onto the pages. Ask to see samples of different types of parent albums available.

Tips to Save Money: Try to negotiate at least one free parents' album with the purchase of the bride and groom's album.

Price Range: $100 - $600

PROOFS/PREVIEWS

Proofs/previews or Proof DVDs are the preliminary prints or digital images from which the bride and groom select photographs for their album and for their parents' albums. The prints vary from 4x5" to 5x5" and 4x6". The DVD allows you to view your photos on a screen in a larger size and more detail.

Things to Consider: When selecting a package, ask how many photos the photographer will take. The more images, the wider the selection you will have to choose from. For a wide selection, the photographer must take at least 3 to 5 times the number of prints that will go into your album.

Ask the photographer how soon after the wedding you will get your proofs. Request this in writing. Ideally, the proofs will be ready by the time you get back from your honeymoon.

Tips to Save Money: Ask your photographer to use your proofs as part of your album package to save developing costs.

Price Range: $100 - $600

DIGITAL FILES

Most digital files are presented as "Jpegs," which is the file type that most labs use to make prints. Your photographer will probably shoot with a professional digital camera that can create extra-large file sizes, which is important for clarity, if you want very large prints made (such as 24x30" and larger).

Things to Consider: Most photographers will not sell you the digital files up front since they hope to make a profit on selling extra prints after the wedding. Ask the photographers you interview how long they keep the files and at what point they will become available to you. A professional photographer should keep a backup copy of the digital files for at least 10 years.

Many photographers will sell you the entire set of digital files after all photos have been ordered by family and friends. Often the price will vary, depending on the amount spent on re-orders. Once you own your digital files, make a back-up copy of your disk every 5 or 6 years, as CDs and DVDs can deteriorate after 8 years or so.

Tips to Save Money: If you can wait, consider contacting the photographer a few years later and ask if s/he will sell you the files at that time. Most photographers will be glad to sell them at a bargain price.

Price Range: $100 - $800

EXTRA PRINTS

Extra prints are photographs ordered in addition to the main album or parents' albums. These are usually purchased as gifts for the bridal party, close friends and family members.

Things to Consider: It is important to discuss the cost of extra prints with your photographer since prices vary considerably. Knowing what extra prints will cost ahead of time will help you know if the photographer is truly within your budget. Think how many extra prints you would like to order and figure this into your budget before selecting a photographer.

Tips to Save Money: If you can wait, consider not ordering any reprints during the first few years after the wedding. A few years later, contact the photographer and ask if s/he will sell you the files. Most photographers will be glad to sell them at a bargain price at a later date. You can then make as many prints as you wish for a fraction of the cost.

Price Range: (5 x 7) = $5.00 - $20; (8 x 10) = $15 - $30; (11 x 14) = $30 - $100

PHOTOGRAPHERS COMPARISON CHART

QUESTIONS	POSSIBILITY 1	POSSIBILITY 2
What is the name and phone number of the photographer?		
What is the website and e-mail of the photographer?		
What is the address of the photographer?		
How many years of experience do you have as a photographer?		
What percentage of your business is dedicated to weddings?		
Approximately how many weddings have you photographed?		
Are you the person who will photograph my wedding?		
Will you bring an assistant with you to my wedding?		
How do you typically dress for weddings?		
Do you have a professional studio?		
What type of equipment do you use?		
Do you bring backup equipment with you to weddings?		
Do you need to visit the ceremony and reception sites prior to the wedding?		
Do you have liability insurance?		
Are you skilled in diffused lighting and soft focus?		
Can you take studio portraits?		
Can you retouch my images?		

POSSIBILITY 3	POSSIBILITY 4	POSSIBILITY 5	POSSIBILITY 6

QUESTIONS	POSSIBILITY 1	POSSIBILITY 2
Can digital files be purchased? If so, what is the cost?		
What is the cost of the package I am interested in?		
What is your payment policy?		
What is your cancellation policy?		
Do you offer a money-back guarantee?		
Do you use paper proofs or DVD proofing?		
How many photographs will I have to choose from?		
When will I get my proofs?		
When will I get my album?		
What is the cost of an engagement portrait?		
What is the cost of a formal bridal portrait?		
What is the cost of a parent album?		
What is the cost of a 5 x 7 reprint?		
What is the cost of an 8 x 10 reprint?		
What is the cost of an 11 x 14 reprint?		
What is the cost per additional hour of shooting at the wedding?		

POSSIBILITY 3	POSSIBILITY 4	POSSIBILITY 5	POSSIBILITY 6

PHOTOGRAPHER'S INFORMATION

Once it is completed, make a copy of this form to give to your photographer as a reminder of your various events.

THE WEDDING OF :   Phone Number:

PHOTOGRAPHER'S COMPANY

Business Name:

Address:

City: State: Zip Code:

Website: E-mail:

Photographer's Name: Phone Number:

Assistant's Name: Phone Number:

ENGAGEMENT PORTRAIT

Date: Time:

Location:

Address:

City: State: Zip Code:

BRIDAL PORTRAIT

Date: Time:

Location:

Address:

City: State: Zip Code:

PHOTOGRAPHER'S INFORMATION

Once it is completed, make a copy of this form to give to your photographer as a reminder of your various events.

OTHER EVENTS

Event:

Date: Time:

Location:

Address:

City: State: Zip Code:

CEREMONY

Date: Arrival Time: Departure Time:

Location:

Address:

City: State: Zip Code:

Ceremony Restrictions/Guidelines:

RECEPTION

Date: Arrival Time: Departure Time:

Location:

Address:

City: State: Zip Code:

Reception Restrictions/Guidelines:

WEDDING PHOTOGRAPHS

Check off all photographs you would like taken throughout your wedding day. Then make a copy of this form and give it to your photographer.

PRE-CEREMONY PHOTOGRAPHS

- ❑ Bride leaving her house
- ❑ Wedding rings with the invitation
- ❑ Bride getting dressed for the ceremony
- ❑ Bride looking at her bridal bouquet
- ❑ Maid of honor putting garter on bride's leg
- ❑ Bride by herself
- ❑ Bride with her mother
- ❑ Bride with her father
- ❑ Bride with mother and father
- ❑ Bride with her entire family and/or any combination thereof
- ❑ Bride with her maid of honor
- ❑ Bride with her bridesmaids
- ❑ Bride with the flower girl and/or ring bearer
- ❑ Bride's mother putting on her corsage
- ❑ Groom leaving his house
- ❑ Groom putting on his boutonniere
- ❑ Groom with his mother
- ❑ Groom with his father
- ❑ Groom with mother and father
- ❑ Groom with his entire family and/or any combination thereof
- ❑ Groom with his best man
- ❑ Groom with his ushers
- ❑ Groom shaking hands with his best man while looking at his watch
- ❑ Groom with the bride's father
- ❑ Bride and her father getting out of the limousine
- ❑ Special members of the family being seated
- ❑ Groom waiting for the bride before the processional
- ❑ Bride and her father just before the processional

Check off all photographs you would like taken throughout your wedding day. Then make a copy of this form and give it to your photographer.

OTHER PRE-CEREMONY PHOTOGRAPHS YOU WOULD LIKE

❑ _____
❑ _____
❑ _____
❑ _____
❑ _____

CEREMONY PHOTOGRAPHS

❑   The processional
❑   Bride and groom saying their vows
❑   Bride and groom exchanging rings
❑   Groom kissing the bride at the altar
❑   The recessional

OTHER CEREMONY PHOTOS YOU WOULD LIKE

❑ _____
❑ _____
❑ _____
❑ _____
❑ _____

POST-CEREMONY PHOTOGRAPHS

❑   Bride and groom
❑   Newlyweds with both of their families
❑   Newlyweds with the entire wedding party
❑   Bride and groom signing the marriage certificate
❑   Flowers and other decorations

OTHER POST-CEREMONY PHOTOS YOU WOULD LIKE

❑ _____
❑ _____
❑ _____
❑ _____
❑ _____

WEDDING PHOTOGRAPHS

Check off all photographs you would like taken throughout your wedding day, then make a copy of this form and give it to your photographer.

RECEPTION PHOTOGRAPHS

- ❑ Entrance of newlyweds and wedding party into the reception site
- ❑ Receiving line
- ❑ Guests signing the guest book
- ❑ Toasts
- ❑ First dance
- ❑ Bride and her father dancing
- ❑ Groom and his mother dancing
- ❑ Bride dancing with groom's father
- ❑ Groom dancing with bride's mother
- ❑ Wedding party and guests dancing
- ❑ Cake table
- ❑ Cake-cutting ceremony
- ❑ Couple feeding each other cake
- ❑ Buffet table and its decoration
- ❑ Bouquet-tossing ceremony
- ❑ Garter-tossing ceremony
- ❑ Musicians
- ❑ The wedding party table
- ❑ The family tables
- ❑ Candid shots of your guests
- ❑ Bride and groom saying good-bye to their parents
- ❑ Bride and groom looking back, waving good-bye in the getaway car

OTHER RECEPTION PHOTOS YOU WOULD LIKE

- ❑ _____
- ❑ _____
- ❑ _____
- ❑ _____
- ❑ _____
- ❑ _____
- ❑ _____
- ❑ _____
- ❑ _____

VIDEOGRAPHY

"There is only one happiness in life,
to love and to be loved."
~ George Sand

MAIN VIDEO 78

TITLES 79

EXTRA HOURS 79

PHOTO MONTAGE... 79

EXTRA COPIES.. 80

VIDEOGRAPHY COMPARISON CHART 82

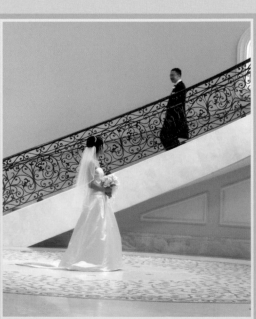

VIDEOGRAPHY

NEXT TO YOUR PHOTO ALBUM, VIDEOGRAPHY IS THE best way to preserve your wedding memories. Unlike photographs, videography captures the mood of the wedding day in motion and sound. Getting a wedding on video used to mean bright lights, cables, microphones and huge obtrusive cameras. But technology has changed, and today's videographers have more advanced equipment that allows them to film ceremonies with minimal disruption.

Today's wedding videos can also be edited and professionally produced, with music, slow motion, black and white scenes and many other special features. You have the option of selecting one, two, or three cameras to record your wedding. The more cameras used, the more action your videographer can capture—and the more expensive the service. An experienced videographer, however, can do a good job with just one camera.

OPTIONS

There are two basic types of wedding video production: documentary and cinematic. The documentary type production records your wedding day as it happened, in real time. Very little editing or embellishment is involved. These types of videos are normally less expensive and can be delivered within days after the wedding.

The cinematic type production is more reminiscent of a movie. Although it can be shot with one camera, most good cinematic wedding videos are shot with two cameras, allowing one videographer to focus on the events as they happen while the other gathers footage that will be added later to enhance the final result. This type of video requires more time due to the extensive editing of the footage, which can take up to 40 hours of studio time.

You may wish to have both of these—one straightforward version and another version with all the details and a nice, theatrical flow.

The latest technology includes the option of producing video in high definition. More televisions are being manufactured with high definition resolution, which delivers a much sharper picture than traditional sets. In years to come, viewers will encounter problems watching regular DVDs on their hi-def television sets. Standard definition video appears fuzzy and pixilated on the new high definition monitors. Having your ceremony shot in high definition will ensure that you'll be able to enjoy watching your wedding video in a crisp, clear resolution for years to come.

MAIN VIDEO

You will need to choose the type of video you want. Do you want the footage edited down to a 30-minute film, or do you want an "as it happened" replay? Remember, an edited video will require more time and will therefore be more expensive than just a documentary of the events.

Things to Consider: Be sure to hire a videographer who specializes in weddings and ask to see samples of his or her work. Weddings are very specialized events. A $1,000 video camera in the hands of a seasoned professional "wedding" videographer will produce far better results than a $3,000 broadcast quality camera or a $4,000 high definition camera in the hands of just an average camera operator. When considering a particular videographer, look at previous weddings the videographer has done. Notice the color and brightness of the screen, as well as the quality of sound. This will indicate the quality of his/her equipment. Note whether the picture is smooth or jerky. This will indicate the videographer's skill level. Ask about special effects such as titles, dissolve, and multiple screens. Find out what's included in the cost of your package so that there are no surprises at the end!

If you will be getting married in a church, find out the church's policies regarding videography. Some churches might require the videographer to film the ceremony from a specific distance.

Beware: As in photography, there are many companies with more than one videographer. These companies may use the work of their best videographer to sell their packages and then send a less experienced videographer to the wedding. Again, don't get caught in this trap! Be sure to interview the videographer who will shoot your wedding so you can get a good idea of his/her style and personality. Ask to see his/her own work.

Tips to Save Money: Compare videographers' quality, value, and price. There is a wide range, and the most expensive is not necessarily the best. The videographer who uses one camera (instead of multiple cameras) is usually the most cost effective and may be all you need.

Consider hiring a company that offers both videography and photography. You might save money by combining the two services.

Ask a family member or close friend to videotape your wedding. However, realize that without professional equipment and expertise, the final product may not be quite as polished.

Price Range: $600 - $4,000

TITLES

Titles and subtitles can be edited into your video before or after the filming. Titles are important since twenty years from now you might not remember the exact time of your wedding or the names of your bridal party members. Some videographers charge more for titling. Make sure you discuss this with your videographer and get in writing exactly what titles will be included.

Options: Titles can include the date, time, and location of the wedding, the bride and groom's names, and the names of special members of the family and bridal party. Titles may also include special thanks to those who helped with the wedding. You can then send these people copies of your video, which would be a very appropriate and inexpensive gift!

Tips to Save Money: Consider asking for limited titles, such as only the names of the bride and groom and the date and time of the wedding.

Price Range: $50 - $300

EXTRA HOURS

Find out how much your videographer would charge to stay longer than the contracted time. Do this in case your reception lasts longer than expected. Don't forget to get this fee in writing.

Tips to Save Money: To avoid paying for hours beyond what's included in your selected package, calculate the maximum number of hours you think you'll need and negotiate that number of hours into your package price.

To reduce the amount of time you'll need to use the videographer, consider recording the ceremony only.

Price Range: $35 - $150 per hour

PHOTO MONTAGE

A photo montage is a series of photographs set to music on video. The number of photographs in your photo montage depends on the length of the songs and the amount of time allotted for each photograph. A typical song usually allows for thirty to forty photographs. Photo montages are a great way to display and reproduce your photographs. Copies of this video can be made for considerably less than the cost of reproducing photos.

VIDEOGRAPHY

Options: Your photo montage can include photos of you and your fiancé growing up in addition to shots from your rehearsal, wedding day, honeymoon, or any combination thereof.

Things to Consider: Send copies of your photo montage video to close friends and family members as mementos of your wedding.

Tips to Save Money: There are many websites on the Internet that allow you to create your own photo montage either for free or at a very low price. You can then transfer your photo montage to a DVD.

Price Range: $60 - $300

EXTRA COPIES

A videographer can produce higher quality copies than you can. Ask your videographer what the charge is for extra copies.

Tips to Save Money: If you have a digital video recorder, you can make copies of your wedding video using a second DVD player. It's easier, however, to burn DVDs on your computer. Before making your own copies of your wedding video, be sure to ask your videographer if that is acceptable. Many contracts prohibit it, and doing so could be copyright infringement. Further, your videographer may have put a security device on the DVD that would prevent you from being able to copy it.

Price Range: $15 - $50

VIDEOGRAPHY COMPARISON CHART

QUESTIONS	POSSIBILITY 1	POSSIBILITY 2
What is the name and phone number of the videographer?		
What is the website and e-mail address of the videographer?		
What is the address of the videographer?		
How many years of experience do you have as a videographer?		
Approximately how many weddings have you videotaped?		
Are you the person who will videotape my wedding?		
Will you bring an assistant with you to my wedding?		
What type of equipment do you use?		
Do you have a wireless microphone?		
Do you bring backup equipment with you?		
Do you visit the ceremony and reception sites before the wedding?		
Do you edit the tape after the event?		
Who keeps the raw footage and for how long?		
When will I receive the final product?		
What is the cost of the desired package?		
What does it include?		
Can you make a photo montage?		
If so, what is your price?		
What is your payment policy?		
What is your cancellation policy?		

POSSIBILITY 3	POSSIBILITY 4	POSSIBILITY 5	POSSIBILITY 6

NOTES

"The best way to show our love is to
give a piece of ourselves to others."
~ Anonymous

INVITATIONS 85

RESPONSE CARDS 90

RECEPTION CARDS 91

CEREMONY CARDS, PEW CARDS................................ 92

SEATING/PLACE CARDS 92

RAIN CARDS, MAPS, CEREMONY PROGRAMS 93

ANNOUNCEMENTS, THANK-YOU NOTES 94

STAMPS, CALLIGRAPHY, NAPKINS/MATCHBOOKS 95

STATIONERY CHECKLIST 97

SAMPLE CEREMONY PROGRAM................................. 98

STATIONERY COMPARISON CHART........................... 100

STATIONERY DESCRIPTION 102

STATIONERY WORDING 103

GUEST AND GIFT LIST 104

ANNOUNCEMENT LIST 105

GUEST ACCOMMODATION LIST 106

ADDRESSING INVITATIONS....................................... 107

GUIDELINES FOR ADDRESSING INVITATIONS............. 108

STATIONERY

PHOTO: KAREN FRENCH

STATIONERY

BEGIN CREATING YOUR GUEST LIST AS SOON AS POSSIBLE. Ask your parents and the groom's parents for a list of people they would like to invite. You and your fiancé should make your own lists. Make certain that all names are spelled correctly and that all addresses are current. Determine if you wish to include children; if so, add their names to your list. All children over the age of 16 should receive their own invitation.

INVITATIONS

Order your invitations at least four months before the wedding. Allow an additional month for engraved invitations. Invitations are traditionally issued by the bride's parents; but if the groom's parents are assuming some of the wedding expenses, the invitations should be in their names also. Mail all invitations at the same time, six to eight weeks before the wedding.

Options: There are three types of invitations: traditional/formal, contemporary, and informal. The traditional/formal wedding invitation is white, soft cream, or ivory with raised black lettering. The printing is done on the top page of a double sheet of thick quality paper; the inside is left blank. The contemporary invitation is typically an individualized presentation that makes a statement about the bride and groom.

Informal invitations are often printed on the front of a single, heavyweight card and may be handwritten or preprinted.

There are three types of printing: engraved, thermography, and offset printing. Engraving is the most expensive, traditional, and formal type of printing. It also takes the longest to complete. In engraved printing, stationery is pressed onto a copper plate, which makes the letters rise slightly from the page. Thermography is a process that fuses powder and ink to create a raised letter. This takes less time than engraving and is less expensive because copper plates do not have to be engraved. Offset printing, the least expensive, is the quickest to produce and offers a variety of styles and colors. It is also the least formal.

STATIONERY

Things to Consider: If all your guests are to be invited to both the ceremony and the reception, a combined invitation may be sent without separate enclosure cards. Order one invitation for each married or cohabiting couple that you plan to invite. The officiant and his/her spouse, as well as your attendants, should receive an invitation.

Order approximately 20 percent more stationery than your actual count. Allow a minimum of two weeks to address and mail the invitations, longer if using a calligrapher or if your guest list is very large. You may also want to consider ordering invitations to the rehearsal dinner, as these should be in the same style as the wedding invitation.

SAMPLES OF TRADITIONAL/FORMAL INVITATIONS

1) When the bride's parents sponsor the wedding:

Mr. and Mrs. Alexander Waterman Smith
request the honor of your presence
at the marriage of their daughter
Carol Ann
to
Mr. William James Clark
on Saturday, the fifth of August
two thousand eight
at two o'clock in the afternoon
Saint James by-the-Sea
La Jolla, California

2) When the groom's parents sponsor the wedding:

Mr. and Mrs. Michael Burdell Clark
request the honor of your presence
at the marriage of
Miss Carol Ann Smith
to their son
Mr. William James Clark

3) When both the bride and groom's parents sponsor the wedding:

Mr. and Mrs. Alexander Waterman Smith
and
Mr. and Mrs. Michael Burdell Clark
request the honor of your presence
at the marriage of their children

Miss Carol Ann Smith
to
Mr. William James Clark

OR

Mr. and Mrs. Alexander Waterman Smith
request the honor of your presence
at the marriage of their daughter
Carol Ann Smith
to
William James Clark
son of Mr. and Mrs. Michael Burdell Clark

4) When the bride and groom sponsor their own wedding:

The honor of your presence is requested
at the marriage of
Miss Carol Ann Smith
and
Mr. William James Clark

OR

Miss Carol Ann Smith
and
Mr. William James Clark
request the honor of your presence
at their marriage

5) With divorced or deceased parents:

a) When the bride's mother is sponsoring the wedding and is not remarried:

Mrs. Julie Hurden Smith
requests the honor of your presence
at the marriage of her daughter
Carol Ann

b) When the bride's mother is sponsoring the wedding and has remarried:

Mrs. Julie Hurden Booker
requests the honor of your presence
at the marriage of her daughter
Carol Ann Smith

OR

Mr. and Mrs. John Thomas Booker
request the honor of your presence
at the marriage of Mrs. Booker's daughter
Carol Ann Smith

c) When the bride's father is sponsoring the wedding and has not remarried:

Mr. Alexander Waterman Smith
requests the honor of your presence
at the marriage of his daughter
Carol Ann

d) When the bride's father is sponsoring the wedding and has remarried:

Mr. and Mrs. Alexander Waterman Smith
request the honor of your presence
at the marriage of Mr. Smith's daughter
Carol Ann

6) With deceased parents:

a) When a close friend or relative sponsors the wedding:

Mr. and Mrs. Brandt Elliott Lawson
request the honor of your presence
at the marriage of their granddaughter
Carol Ann Smith

7) In military ceremonies, the rank determines the placement of names:

a) Any title lower than sergeant should be omitted. Only the branch of service should be included under that person's name:

Mr. and Mrs. Alexander Waterman Smith
request the honor of your presence
at the marriage of their daughter
Carol Ann
to
William James Clark
United States Army

b) Junior officers' titles are placed below their names and are followed by their branch of service:

Mr. and Mrs. Alexander Waterman Smith
request the honor of your presence
at the marriage of their daughter
Carol Ann
to
William James Clark
First Lieutenant, United States Army

c) If the rank is higher than lieutenant, titles are placed before names, and the branch of service is placed on the following line:

Mr. and Mrs. Alexander Waterman Smith
request the honor of your presence
at the marriage of their daughter
Carol Ann
to
Captain William James Clark
United States Navy

SAMPLE OF A LESS FORMAL/MORE CONTEMPORARY INVITATION

Mr. and Mrs. Alexander Waterman Smith
would like you to
join with their daughter
Carol Ann
and
William James Clark
in the celebration of their marriage

For additional wording suggestions, log on to www.WeddingSolutions.com

STATIONERY

Tips to Save Money: Thermography looks like engraving and is one-third the cost. Choose paper stock that is reasonable and yet achieves your overall look. Select invitations that can be mailed using just one stamp. Order at least 25 extra invitations in case you soil some or add people to your list. To reorder this small number of invitations later would cost nearly three times the amount you'll spend up front.

Price Range: $0.75 - $6 per invitation

RESPONSE CARDS

Response cards are enclosed with the invitation to determine the number of people who will be attending your wedding. They are the smallest card size accepted by the postal service and should be printed in the same style as the invitation. An invitation to only the wedding ceremony does not usually include a request for a reply. However, response cards should be used when it is necessary to have an exact head count for special seating arrangements. Response cards are widely accepted today. If included, these cards should be easy for your guests to understand and use. Include a self-addressed and stamped return envelope to make it easy for your guests to return the response cards.

Things to Consider: You should not include a line that reads "number of persons" on your response cards because only those whose names appear on the inner and outer envelopes are invited. Each couple, each single person, and all children over the age of 16 should receive their own invitation. Indicate on the inner envelope if they may bring an escort or guest. The omitting of children's names from the inner envelope infers that the children are not invited.

Samples of wording for response cards:

M_____

(The M may be eliminated from the line, especially if many Drs. are invited)

___ accepts

___ regrets

Saturday the fifth of July

Oceanside Country Club

OR

The favor of your reply is requested

by the twenty-second of May

M_____

will _____ attend

Price Range: $0.40 - $1 each

RECEPTION CARDS

If the guest list for the ceremony is larger than that for the reception, a separate card with the date, time and location for the reception should be enclosed with the ceremony invitation for those guests also invited to the reception. Reception cards should be placed in front of the invitation, facing the back flap and the person inserting them. They should be printed on the same quality paper and in the same style as the invitation itself.

Sample of a formally worded reception card:

> Mr. and Mrs. Alexander Waterman Smith
> request the pleasure of your company
> Saturday, the third of July
> at three o'clock
> Oceanside Country Club
> 2020 Waterview Lane
> Oceanside, California

Sample of a less formal reception card:

> Reception immediately following the ceremony
> Oceanside Country Club
> 2020 Waterview Lane
> Oceanside, California

Things to Consider: You may also include a reception card in all your invitations if the reception is to be held at a different site than the ceremony.

Tips to Save Money: If all people invited to the ceremony are also invited to the reception, include the reception information on the invitation and eliminate the reception card. This will save printing and postage costs.

Price Range: $0.40 - $1 each

For additional wording suggestions, log on to www.WeddingSolutions.com

STATIONERY

CEREMONY CARDS

If the guest list for the reception is larger than the guest list for the ceremony, a special insertion card with the date, time, and location for the ceremony should be enclosed with the reception invitation for those guests also invited to the ceremony.

Ceremony cards should be placed in front of the invitation, facing the back flap and the person inserting them. They should be printed on the same quality paper and in the same style as the invitation itself.

Price Range: $0.40 - $1 each

PEW CARDS

Pew cards may be used to let special guests and family members know they are to be seated in the reserved section on either the bride's side or the groom's side. These are most typically seen in large, formal ceremonies. Guests should take this card to the ceremony and show it to the ushers, who should then escort them to their seats.

Options: Pew cards may indicate a specific pew number if specific seats are assigned, or may read "Within the Ribbon" if certain pews are reserved, but no specific seat is assigned.

Things to Consider: Pew cards may be inserted along with the invitation, or may be sent separately after the RSVPs have been returned. It is often easier to send them after you have received all RSVPs so you know how many reserved pews will be needed.

Tips to Save Money: Include the pew card with the invitation to special guests and just say, "Within the Ribbon." After you have received all your RSVPs, you will know how many pews need to be reserved. This will save you the cost of mailing the pew cards separately.

Price Range: $0.25 - $1 each

SEATING/PLACE CARDS

Seating/place cards are used to let guests know where they should be seated at the reception and are a good way of putting people together so they feel most comfortable. Place cards should be laid out alphabetically on a table at the entrance to the reception. Each card should correspond to a table—either by number, color, or other identifying factor. Each table should be marked accordingly.

Options: Select a traditional or contemporary design for your place cards, depending on the style of your wedding.

Regardless of the design, place cards must contain the same information: the bride and groom's names on the first line; the date on the second line; the third line is left blank for you to write in the guest's name; and the fourth line is for the table number, color, or other identifying factor.

Price Range: $0.25 - $1 each

RAIN CARDS

These cards are enclosed when guests are invited to an outdoor ceremony and/or reception, informing them of an alternate location in case of bad weather. As with other enclosures, rain cards should be placed in front of the invitation, facing the back flap and the person inserting them. They should be printed on the same quality paper and in the same style as the invitation itself.

Price Range: $0.25 - $1 each

MAPS

Maps to the ceremony and/or reception are becoming frequent inserts in wedding invitations. They need to be drawn and printed in the same style as the invitation and are usually on a small, heavier card. If they are not printed in the same style or on the same type of paper as the invitation, they should be mailed separately.

Options: Maps should include both written and visual instructions, keeping in mind the fact that guests may be coming from different locations.

Things to Consider: Order extra maps to hand out at the ceremony if the reception is at a different location.

Tips to Save Money: If you are comfortable with computers, you can purchase software that allows you to draw your own maps. Print a map to both the ceremony and reception on the same sheet of paper, perhaps one on each side. This will save you the cost of mailing two maps. Or have your ushers hand out maps to the reception after the ceremony.

Price Range: $0.50 - $1 each

CEREMONY PROGRAMS

Ceremony programs are printed documents showing the sequence of events during the ceremony. These programs add a personal touch to your wedding and are a convenient way of letting guests know who your attendants, officiant, and ceremony musicians are.

STATIONERY

Options: Ceremony programs can be handed out by the ushers, or they can be placed at the back of the church for guests to take as they enter.

Price Range: $0.75 - $3 each

ANNOUNCEMENTS

Announcements are not obligatory but serve a useful purpose. They may be sent to friends who are not invited to the wedding because the number of guests must be limited or because they live too far away. They may also be sent to acquaintances who, while not particularly close to the family, might still wish to know about the marriage.

Announcements are also appropriate for friends and acquaintances who are not expected to attend and for whom you do not want to give an obligation of sending a gift. They should include the day, month, year, city, and state where the ceremony took place.

Things to Consider: Announcements should never be sent to anyone who has received an invitation to the ceremony or the reception. They are printed on the same paper and in the same style as the invitation. They should be addressed before the wedding and mailed the day of or the day after the ceremony.

Price Range: $0.75 - $2 each

THANK-YOU NOTES

Regardless of whether the bride has thanked the donor in person or not, she must write a thank-you note for every gift received.

Things to Consider: Order thank-you notes along with your other stationery at least four months before your wedding. You should order some with your maiden initials for thank-you notes sent before the ceremony, and the rest with your married initials for notes sent after the wedding and for future use. Send thank-you notes within two weeks of receiving a gift that arrives before the wedding, and within two months after the honeymoon for gifts received on or after your wedding day. Be sure to mention the gift you received in the body of the note and let the person know how much you like it and what you plan to do with it.

Price Range: $0.40 - $0.75 each

STAMPS

Don't forget to budget stamps for response cards as well as for invitations!

Things to Consider: Don't order stamps until you have had the post office weigh your completed invitation. It may exceed the size and weight for one stamp. Order commemorative stamps that fit the occasion.

Price Range: $0.39 - $1 per each invitation

CALLIGRAPHY

Calligraphy is a form of elegant handwriting often used to address invitations for formal occasions. Traditional wedding invitations should be addressed in black or blue fountain pen.

Options: You may address the invitations yourself, hire a professional calligrapher, or have your invitations addressed using calligraphy by computer. Make sure you use the same method or person to address both the inner and outer envelopes.

Tips to Save Money: You may want to consider taking a short course to learn the art of calligraphy so that you can address your own invitations. If you have a computer with a laser printer, you can address the invitations yourself using one of many beautiful calligraphy fonts.

Price Range: $0.50 - $3 each

NAPKINS/MATCHBOOKS

Napkins and matchbooks may also be ordered from your stationer. These are placed around the reception room as decorative items and mementos of the event.

Things to Consider: Napkins and matchbooks can be printed in your wedding colors, or simply white with gold or silver lettering. Include both of your names and the wedding date. You may consider including a phrase or thought, or a small graphic design above your names.

Price Range: $0.50 - $1.50 each

NOTES

STATIONERY ITEM	Quantity	Cost
❏ Invitations		
❏ Envelopes		
❏ Response Cards/Envelopes		
❏ Reception Cards		
❏ Ceremony Cards		
❏ Pew Cards		
❏ Seating/Place Cards		
❏ Rain Cards		
❏ Maps		
❏ Ceremony Programs		
❏ Announcements		
❏ Thank-You Notes		
❏ Stamps		
❏ Personalized Napkins/Matchbooks		
❏ Other:		
❏ Other:		
❏ Other:		

SAMPLE CEREMONY PROGRAM

The Marriage of
Carol Ann Smith and William James Clark
the eleventh of March, 2008
San Diego, California

OUR CEREMONY

Prelude:
All I Ask of You, by Andrew Lloyd Webber

Processional:
Canon in D Major, by Pachelbel

Rite of Marriage

Welcome guests

Statement of intentions

Marriage vows

Exchange of rings

Blessing of bride and groom

Pronouncement of marriage

Presentation of the bride and groom

Recessional:
Trumpet Voluntary, by Jeromiah Clarke

OUR WEDDING PARTY

Maid of Honor:
Susan Smith, Sister of Bride

Best Man:
Brandt Clark, Brother of Groom

Bridesmaids:
Janet Anderson, Friend of Bride
Lisa Bennett, Friend of Bride

Ushers:
Mark Gleason, Friend of Groom
Tommy Olson, Friend of Groom

Officiant:
Father Henry Thomas

OUR RECEPTION

Please join us after the ceremony
in the celebration of our marriage at:
La Valencia Hotel
1132 Prospect Street
La Jolla, California

STATIONERY COMPARISON CHART

QUESTIONS	POSSIBILITY 1	POSSIBILITY 2
What is the name and phone number of the stationery provider?		
What is the website and e-mail of the stationery provider?		
What is the address of the stationery provider?		
How many years of experience do you have?		
What lines of stationery do you carry?		
What types of printing processes do you offer?		
How soon in advance does the order have to be placed?		
What is the turnaround time?		
What is the cost of the desired invitation? Announcement?		
What is the cost of the desired response card? Reception card?		
What is the cost of the desired thank-you note?		
What is the cost of the desired party favors?		
What is the cost of the desired wedding program?		
What is the cost of addressing the envelopes in calligraphy?		
What is your payment policy?		
What is your cancellation policy?		

POSSIBILITY 3	POSSIBILITY 4	POSSIBILITY 5	POSSIBILITY 6

STATIONERY DESCRIPTION

STATIONER: _____   Date Ordered: _____

Salesperson: _____   Phone Number: _____

Address: _____

City: _____   State: _____   Zip Code: _____

Website: _____

E-mail: _____

STATIONERY ITEM: (Include selections for Paper, Style, Color, Font, Printing)

Invitations/Envelopes: _____

Response Cards/Envelopes: _____

Reception Cards: _____

Ceremony Cards: _____

Pew Cards: _____

Seating/Place Cards: _____

Rain Cards: _____

Maps: _____

Ceremony Programs: _____

Announcements: _____

Thank-You Notes: _____

Napkins: _____

Matchbooks: _____

Invitations:
_____
_____
_____
_____
_____
_____

Announcements:
_____
_____
_____
_____
_____

Reception Cards:
_____
_____

Response Cards:
_____
_____

Seating/Place Cards:
_____
_____

Napkins/Matchbooks:
_____
_____
_____
_____

GUEST AND GIFT LIST

Make as many copies of this form as needed.

Name:

Address:

City:

State: Zip Code:

Phone Number:

Email:

Table/Pew #:

Shower Gift:

❑ Thank-You Note Sent

Wedding Gift:

❑ Thank-You Note Sent

Name:

Address:

City:

State: Zip Code:

Phone Number:

Email:

Table/Pew #:

Shower Gift:

❑ Thank-You Note Sent

Wedding Gift:

❑ Thank-You Note Sent

Name:

Address:

City:

State: Zip Code:

Phone Number:

Email:

Table/Pew #:

Shower Gift:

❑ Thank-You Note Sent

Wedding Gift:

❑ Thank-You Note Sent

Name:

Address:

City:

State: Zip Code:

Phone Number:

Email:

Table/Pew #:

Shower Gift:

❑ Thank-You Note Sent

Wedding Gift:

❑ Thank-You Note Sent

Name:

Address:

City:

State: Zip Code:

Phone Number:

Email:

Table/Pew #:

Shower Gift:

❑ Thank-You Note Sent

Wedding Gift:

❑ Thank-You Note Sent

Name:

Address:

City:

State: Zip Code:

Phone Number:

Email:

Table/Pew #:

Shower Gift:

❑ Thank-You Note Sent

Wedding Gift:

❑ Thank-You Note Sent

Make as many copies of this form as needed.

Name:

Address:

City:

State: Zip Code:

Phone Number:

Email:

Name:

Address:

City:

State: Zip Code:

Phone Number:

Email:

Name:

Address:

City:

State: Zip Code:

Phone Number:

Email:

Name:

Address:

City:

State: Zip Code:

Phone Number:

Email:

Name:

Address:

City:

State: Zip Code:

Phone Number:

Email:

Name:

Address:

City:

State: Zip Code:

Phone Number:

Email:

Name:

Address:

City:

State: Zip Code:

Phone Number:

Email:

Name:

Address:

City:

State: Zip Code:

Phone Number:

Email:

GUEST ACCOMMODATION LIST

Make as many copies of this form as needed to accommodate the size of your guest list.

Name: _____ Phone Number: _____
Arrival Date: _____ Time: _____ Cost Per Room: _____
Airline/Train: _____ Confirmation No.: _____
Flight/Train No.: _____ Departure Date: _____ Time: _____
Pick Up By: _____ Taken By: _____
Will Stay At: _____ Airline/Train: _____
Address: _____ Flight/Train No.: _____

Name: _____ Phone Number: _____
Arrival Date: _____ Time: _____ Cost Per Room: _____
Airline/Train: _____ Confirmation No.: _____
Flight/Train No.: _____ Departure Date: _____ Time: _____
Pick Up By: _____ Taken By: _____
Will Stay At: _____ Airline/Train: _____
Address: _____ Flight/Train No.: _____

Name: _____ Phone Number: _____
Arrival Date: _____ Time: _____ Cost Per Room: _____
Airline/Train: _____ Confirmation No.: _____
Flight/Train No.: _____ Departure Date: _____ Time: _____
Pick Up By: _____ Taken By: _____
Will Stay At: _____ Airline/Train: _____
Address: _____ Flight/Train No.: _____

Name: _____ Phone Number: _____
Arrival Date: _____ Time: _____ Cost Per Room: _____
Airline/Train: _____ Confirmation No.: _____
Flight/Train No.: _____ Departure Date: _____ Time: _____
Pick Up By: _____ Taken By: _____
Will Stay At: _____ Airline/Train: _____
Address: _____ Flight/Train No.: _____

Name: _____ Phone Number: _____
Arrival Date: _____ Time: _____ Cost Per Room: _____
Airline/Train: _____ Confirmation No.: _____
Flight/Train No.: _____ Departure Date: _____ Time: _____
Pick Up By: _____ Taken By: _____
Will Stay At: _____ Airline/Train: _____
Address: _____ Flight/Train No.: _____

ADDRESSING INVITATIONS

WE RECOMMEND THAT YOU START ADDRESSING YOUR invitations at least three months before your wedding, and preferably four months if you are using calligraphy or if your guest list is above 200. You may want to ask your maid of honor or bridesmaids to help you with this time-consuming task, as this is traditionally part of their responsibilities. Organize a luncheon or late afternoon get together with hors d'oeuvres and make a party out of it! If you are working with a wedding consultant, s/he can also help you address invitations.

There are typically two envelopes that need to be addressed for wedding invitations: an inner envelope and an outer envelope. The inner envelope is placed unsealed inside the outer envelope, with the flap away from the person inserting.

The invitation and all enclosures are placed inside the inner envelope facing the back flap. The inner envelope contains the name (or names) of the person (or people) who are invited to the ceremony and/or reception. The address is not included on the inner envelope.

The outer envelope contains the name (or names) and address of the person (or people) to whom the inner envelope belongs.

Use the guidelines on the following page to help you properly address both the inner and outer envelopes.

GUIDELINES FOR ADDRESSING INVITATIONS

SITUATION	INNER ENVELOPE No first name or address	OUTER ENVELOPE Has first name & address
Husband and Wife (with same surname)	Mr. and Mrs. Smith	Mr. and Mrs. Thomas Smith (use middle name, if known)
Husband and Wife (with different surnames)	Ms. Banks and Mr. Smith (wife first)	Ms. Anita Banks Mr. Thomas Smith (wife's name & title above husband's)
Husband and Wife (wife has professional title)	Dr. Smith and Mr. Smith	Dr. Anita Smith Mr. Thomas Smith (wife's name & title above husband's)
Husband and Wife (with children under 16)	Mr. and Mrs. Smith John, Mary, and Glen (in order of age)	Mr. and Mrs. Thomas Smith
Single Woman (regardless of age)	Miss/Ms. Smith	Miss/Ms. Beverly Smith
Single Woman and Guest	Miss/Ms. Smith Mr. Jones (or "and Guest")	Miss/Ms. Beverly Smith
Single Man	Mr. Jones (Master for a young boy)	Mr. William Jones
Single Man and Guest	Mr. Jones Miss/Ms. Smith (or "and Guest")	Mr. William Jones
Unmarried Couple Living Together	Mr. Knight and Ms. Orlandi (names listed alphabetically)	Mr. Michael Knight Ms. Paula Orlandi
Two Sisters (over 16)	The Misses Smith	The Misses Mary and Jane Smith (in order of age)
Two Brothers (over 16)	The Messrs. Smith	The Messrs. John and Glen Smith (in order of age)
Brothers & Sisters (over 16)	Mary, Jane, John & Glen (name the girls first, in order of age)	The Misses Smith The Messrs. Smith (name the girls first)
A Brother and Sister (over 16)	Jane and John (name the girl first)	Miss Jane Smith and Mr. John Smith (name the girl first)
Widow	Mrs. Smith	Mrs. William Smith
Divorcee	Mrs. Smith	Mrs. Jones Smith (maiden name and former husband's surname)

"To get the full value of joy, you must have someone to divide it with."
~ Mark Twain

RECEPTION

RECEPTION SITE FEE 109

HORS D'OEUVRES, MAIN MEAL/CATERER 110

LIQUOR/BEVERAGES 112

BARTENDING/BAR SET-UP FEE 113

CORKAGE FEE, FEE TO POUR COFFEE 114

SERVICE PROVIDERS' MEALS 114

GRATUITY 115

PARTY FAVORS, DISPOSABLE CAMERAS 115

ROSE PETALS/RICE 116

GIFT ATTENDANT 117

PARKING FEE/VALET SERVICES 117

RECEPTION SITE COMPARISON CHART 118

RECEPTION SITE INFORMATION SHEET 122

CATERER INFORMATION SHEET 123

TABLE SEATING ARRANGEMENTS 124

LIQUOR ORDER FORM 126

PARTY FAVORS COMPARISON CHART 127

CATERER COMPARISON CHART 128

MENU WORKSHEET 130

PHOTO: KAREN FRENCH

RECEPTION

THE RECEPTION IS A PARTY WHERE ALL YOUR GUESTS come together to celebrate your new life as a married couple. It should reflect and complement the formality of your ceremony. The selection of a reception site will depend on its availability, price, proximity to the ceremony site, and the number of people it will accommodate.

RECEPTION SITE FEE

There are two basic types of reception sites. The first type charges a per person fee that includes the facility, food, tables, silverware, china, and so forth. Examples: hotels, restaurants, and catered yachts. The second type charges a room rental fee and you are responsible for providing the food, beverages, linens, and possibly tables and chairs. Examples: clubs, halls, parks, museums, and private homes.

The advantage of the first type is that almost everything is done for you. The disadvantage, however, is that your choices of food, china, and linen are limited. Usually you are not permitted to bring in an outside caterer and must select from a predetermined menu.

Options: Private homes, gardens, hotels, clubs, restaurants, halls, parks, museums, yachts, and wineries are some of the more popular choices for receptions.

Things to Consider: When comparing the cost of different locations, consider the rental fee, food, beverages, parking, gratuity, setup charges, and the cost of rental equipment needed such as tables, chairs, canopies, and so forth. If you are planning an outdoor reception, be sure to have a backup site in case of rain.

Beware: Some hotels are known for double booking. A bride may reserve the largest or most elegant room in a hotel for her reception, only to find out later that the hotel took the liberty to book a more profitable event in the room she had reserved and moved her reception over to a smaller or less elegant room.

Also be careful of hotels that book events too close together. You don't want your guests to wait outside while your room is being set up for the reception. And you don't want to be "forced out" before you are ready to leave because the hotel needs

RECEPTION

to arrange the room for the next reception. Get your rental hours and the name of your room in writing.

Tips to Save Money: Since the cost of the reception is approximately 35% of the total cost of your wedding, you can save the most money by limiting your guest list. If you hire a wedding consultant, s/he may be able to cut your cake and save you the cake-cutting fee. Check this out with your facility or caterer. Reception sites that charge a room rental fee may waive this fee if you meet minimum requirements on food and beverages consumed. Try to negotiate this before you book the facility.

Price Range: $300 - $5,000

HORS D'OEUVRES

At receptions where a full meal is to be served, hors d'oeuvres may be offered to guests during the first hour of the reception. However, at a tea or cocktail reception, hors d'oeuvres will be the "main course."

Options: There are many options for hors d'oeuvres, depending on the formality of your reception and the type of food to be served at the meal. Popular items are foods that can easily be picked up and eaten with one hand. Hors d'oeuvres may be set out on tables "buffet style" for guests to help themselves, or they may be passed around on trays by waiters and waitresses.

Things to Consider: When selecting hors d'oeuvres for your reception, consider whether heating or refrigeration will be available and choose your food accordingly. When planning your menu, consider the time of day. You should select lighter hors d'oeuvres for a midday reception and heavier hors d'oeuvres for an evening reception.

Tips to Save Money: Tray pass hors d'oeuvres during cocktail hour and serve a lighter meal. Avoid serving hors d'oeuvres that are labor intensive or that require expensive ingredients. Compare two or three caterers; there is a wide price range between caterers for the same food. Compare the total cost of catering (main entree plus hors d'oeuvres) when selecting a caterer. Consider serving hors d'oeuvres buffet style. Your guests will eat less this way than if waiters and waitresses are constantly serving them hors d'oeuvres.

Price Range: $3 - $20 per person

MAIN MEAL/CATERER

If your reception is going to be at a hotel, restaurant or other facility that provides food, you will need to select a meal to serve your guests. Most of these facilities will have a predetermined menu from which to select your meal. If your reception is going to be in a facility that does not provide food, you will need to hire an outside caterer. The caterer will be responsible for preparing, cooking, and serving the food. The caterer will also be responsible for beverages and for cleaning up after the event. Before signing a contract, make sure you understand all the services the caterer will provide. Your contract should state the amount and type of food and beverages that will be served, the way in which they will be served, the number of servers who will be available, and the cost per food item or person.

Options: Food can be served either buffet style or as a sit-down meal. It should be chosen according to the time of day, year, and formality of the wedding. Although there are many main dishes to choose from, chicken and beef are the most popular selections for a large event. Ask your facility manager or caterer for their specialty. If you have a special type of food you would like to serve at your reception, select a facility or caterer who specializes in preparing it.

Things to Consider: When hiring a caterer, check to see if the location for your reception provides refrigeration and cooking equipment. If not, make sure your caterer is fully self-supported with portable refrigeration and heating equipment. A competent caterer will prepare much of the food in his/her own kitchen and should provide an adequate staff of cooks, servers, and bartenders. Ask for references and look at photos from previous parties so you know how the food will be presented; or better yet, visit an event they are catering.

Beware: Avoid mayonnaise, cream sauces, or custard fillings if food must go unrefrigerated for any length of time.

Tips to Save Money: Give only 85 to 95 percent of your final guest count to your caterer or facility manager, depending on how certain you are that all of your guests who have responded will come. Chances are that several, if not many, of your guests will not show up. But if they do, your caterer should have enough food for all of them. This is especially true with buffet-style receptions, in which case the facility or caterer will charge extra for each additional guest. However, if you give a complete count of your guests to your caterer and some of them don't show up, you will still have to pay for their plates. If offering a buffet meal, have the catering staff serve the food onto guests' plates rather than allowing guests to serve themselves. This will help to regulate the amount of food consumed.

Select food that is not too time-consuming to prepare, or food that does not have expensive ingredients. Also, consider a brunch or early afternoon wedding so the reception will fall between meals, allowing you to serve hors d'oeuvres instead of a full meal. Or tray pass hors d'oeuvres during cocktail hour and choose a lighter meal.

Price Range: $20 - $100 per person

RECEPTION

LIQUOR/BEVERAGES

Prices for liquor and beverages vary greatly, depending on the amount and brand of alcohol served. Traditionally, at least champagne or punch should be served to toast the couple.

Options: White and red wines, scotch, vodka, gin, rum, and beer are the most popular alcoholic beverages. Sodas and fruit punch are popular nonalcoholic beverages served at receptions. And of course, don't forget coffee or tea. There are a number of options and variations for serving alcoholic beverages: a full open bar where you pay for your guests to drink as much as they wish; an open bar for the first hour, followed by a cash bar where guests pay for their own drinks; cash bar only; beer and wine only; nonalcoholic beverages only; or any combination thereof.

Things to Consider: If you plan to serve alcoholic beverages at a reception site that does not provide liquor, make sure your caterer has a license to serve alcohol and that your reception site allows alcoholic beverages. If you plan to order your own alcohol, do so three or four weeks before the event. If you plan to have a no-host or "cash" bar, consider notifying your guests so they know to bring cash with them. A simple line that says "No-Host Bar" on the reception card should suffice.

In selecting the type of alcohol to serve, consider the age and preference of your guests, the type of food that will be served, and the time of day your guests will be drinking.

On the average, you should allow one drink per person, per hour at the reception. A bottle of champagne will usually serve six glasses. Never serve liquor without some type of food. Use the following chart to plan your beverage needs:

Beverages	Amount based on 100 guests
Bourbon	3 Fifths
Gin	3 Fifths
Rum	2 Fifths
Scotch	4 Quarts
Vodka	5 Quarts
White Wine	2 Cases
Red Wine	1 Case
Champagne	3 Cases
Other	2 Cases each: Club Soda, Seltzer Water, Tonic Water, Ginger Ale, Cola, Beer

If you are hosting an open bar at a hotel or restaurant, ask the catering manager how they charge for liquor: by consumption or by number of bottles opened. Get this in writing before the event and then ask for a full consumption report after the event.

Beware: In today's society, it is not uncommon for the hosts of a party to be held legally responsible for the conduct and safety of their guests. Keep this in mind when planning the quantity and type of beverages to serve. Also, be sure to remind your bartenders not to serve alcohol to minors.

Tips to Save Money: To keep beverage costs down, serve punch, wine, or nonalcoholic drinks only. If your caterer allows it, consider buying liquor from a wholesaler who will let you return unopened bottles. Also, avoid salty foods such as potato chips, pretzels, or ham. These foods will make your guests thirstier so they will tend to drink more.

Host alcoholic beverages for the first hour, then go to a cash bar. Or host beer, wine, and soft drinks only and have mixed drinks available on a cash basis. The bartending fee is often waived if you meet the minimum requirements on beverages consumed. For the toast, tray pass champagne only to those guests who want it, not to everyone. Many people will make a toast with whatever they are currently drinking. Consider serving sparkling cider in place of champagne.

Omit waiters and waitresses. Instead, have an open bar in which your guests have to get their own drinks. People tend to drink almost twice as much if there are waiters and waitresses constantly asking them if they would like another drink and then bringing drinks to them.

Price Range: $8 - $35 per person

BARTENDING/BAR SETUP FEE

Some reception sites and caterers charge an extra fee for bartending and for setting up the bar.

Tips to Save Money: The bartending fee could be and often is waived if you meet a minimum requirement on beverages consumed. Try to negotiate this with your caterer prior to hiring him/her.

Price Range: $75 - $500

RECEPTION

CORKAGE FEE

Many reception sites and caterers make money by marking up the food and alcohol they sell. You may wish to provide your own alcohol for several reasons. First, it is more cost effective. Second, you may want to serve an exotic wine or champagne that the reception site or caterer does not offer. In either case, and if your reception site or caterer allows it, be prepared to pay a corkage fee. This is the fee for each bottle brought into the reception site and opened by a member of their staff.

Things to Consider: You need to consider whether the expenses saved after paying the corkage fee justify the hassle and liability of bringing in your own alcohol.

Price Range: $5 - $20 per bottle

FEE TO POUR COFFEE

In addition to corkage and cake-cutting fees, some facilities also charge extra to pour coffee with the wedding cake.

Things to Consider: Again, when comparing the cost of various reception sites, don't forget to add up all the extra miscellaneous costs, such as the fee for pouring coffee.

Price Range: $0.25 - $1 per person

SERVICE PROVIDERS' MEALS

Things to Consider: It is considered a courtesy to feed your photographer, videographer, and any other "service provider" at the reception. Check options and prices with your caterer or reception site manager. Make sure you allocate a place for your service providers to eat. You may want them to eat with your guests, or you may prefer setting a place outside the main room for them to eat. Your service providers may be more comfortable with the latter.

Tips to Save Money: You don't need to feed your service providers the same meal as your guests. You can order sandwiches or another less expensive meal for them. If the meal is a buffet, there should be enough food left after all your guests have been served for your service providers to eat. Tell them they are welcome to eat after all your guests have been served. Be sure to discuss this with your catering manager.

Price Range: $10 - $30 per person

GRATUITY

It is customary to pay a gratuity fee to your caterer. The average gratuity is 15 percent to 20 percent of your food and beverage bill.

Tips to Save Money: Ask about these costs up front and select your caterer or reception site accordingly.

Price Range: 15 - 25 percent of total food and beverage bill

PARTY FAVORS

Party favors are little gift items given to your guests as mementos of your wedding. They add a very special touch to your wedding and can become keepsakes for your guests.

Options: White matchboxes engraved with the couple's names and wedding date; cocktail napkins marked in the same way; individually wrapped and marked chocolates, almonds, or fine candy are all popular party favors. Wine or champagne bottles marked with the bride and groom's names and wedding date on a personalized label are also very popular. These come in different sizes and can be purchased by the case.

If you can afford it, you may also consider porcelain or ceramic party favors. These can be custom-fired with your name and wedding date on them. A new idea that's gaining in popularity among environmentally conscientious couples is to present each guest with a tiny shoot of an endangered tree to be planted in honor of the bride and groom.

Things to Consider: Personalized favors need to be ordered several weeks in advance.

Price Range: $1 - $25 per person

DISPOSABLE CAMERAS

A great way to inexpensively obtain many candid photographs of your wedding day is to place a disposable 35mm camera loaded with film on each table at your reception, and to have your guests take shots of the event! Disposable cameras come pre loaded with film. Your guests can leave the cameras at their table or drop them in a basket or other labeled container near the entrance to the reception site. Arrange for someone to collect the cameras after the event. Tell your DJ, musician, or wedding coordinator to encourage your guests to take photographs with the disposables. You will end up with many beautiful, memorable and candid photographs of your reception.

RECEPTION

Things to Consider: Disposable cameras are sold with and without flash. Disposable cameras with flash are more expensive but necessary if your reception is going to be held indoors or in the evening. If you are planning a large reception, consider buying cameras with only twelve exposures. Otherwise, you may end up with too many photographs. For example, if 200 guests attend your reception and you seat eight guests per table, you will need to purchase 25 cameras. If each camera has 36 exposures, you will end up with 825 photographs. If the cameras have only twelve exposures, you will end up with 300 photographs, which is a much more reasonable quantity!

Tips to Save Money: Instead of developing these photographs into print and then placing them into a big album, have your videographer transfer the negatives directly onto video set to your favorite music. You can then reproduce this "photo montage" and send it as a gift to your friends and family members. You can later decide which of these photographs you want to develop into print.

Price Range: $4 - $20 per camera

ROSE PETALS/RICE

Rose petals or rice are traditionally tossed over the bride and groom as they leave the church after the ceremony or when they leave the reception. These are usually handed out to guests in little sachet bags while the bride and groom are changing into their going away clothes. This tradition was initiated in the Middle Ages whereby a handful of wheat was thrown over the bridal couple as a symbol of fertility. Rose petals are used to symbolize happiness, beauty, and prosperity.

Options: Rose petals, rice, or confetti is often used. However, an environmentally correct alternative is to use grass or flower seeds, which do not need to be "cleaned up" if tossed over a grassy area. These come wrapped in attractive, recycled packages with the couple's names and wedding date printed on the front.

Things to Consider: Rose petals can stain carpets; rice can sting faces, harm birds and make stairs dangerously slippery; confetti is messy and hard to clean. Clubs and hotels seldom permit the use of any of these. Ask about their policy.

Price Range: $0.35 - $2 per person

GIFT ATTENDANT

The gift attendant is responsible for watching over your gifts during the reception so that no one walks away with them. This is necessary only if your reception is held in a public area such as a hotel or outside garden where strangers may be walking by. It is not proper to have a friend or family member take on this duty as s/he would not enjoy the reception. The gift attendant should also be responsible for transporting your gifts from the reception site to your car or bridal suite.

Tips to Save Money: Hire a young boy or girl from your neighborhood to watch over your gifts at the reception.

Price Range: $20 - $100

PARKING FEE/VALET SERVICES

Many reception sites such as hotels, restaurants, etc., charge for parking. It is customary, although not necessary, for the host of the wedding to pay this charge. At a large home reception, you should consider hiring a professional, qualified valet service if parking could be a problem. If so, make sure the valet service is fully insured.

Things to Consider: When comparing the cost of reception sites, don't forget to add the cost of parking to the total price.

Tips to Save Money: To save money, let your guests pay their own parking fees.

Price Range: $3 - $10 per car

RECEPTION SITE COMPARISON CHART

QUESTIONS	POSSIBILITY 1	POSSIBILITY 2
What is the name of the reception site?		
What is the website and e-mail of the reception site?		
What is the address of the reception site?		
What is the name and phone number of my contact person?		
What dates and times are available?		
What is the maximum number of guests for a seated reception?		
What is the maximum number of guests for a cocktail reception?		
What is the reception site fee?		
What is the price range for a seated lunch?		
What is the price range for a buffet lunch?		
What is the price range for a seated dinner?		
What is the price range for a buffet dinner?		
What is the corkage fee?		
What is the cake-cutting fee?		
What is the ratio of servers to guests?		
How much time will be allotted for my reception?		
What music restrictions are there, if any?		
What alcohol restrictions are there, if any?		

POSSIBILITY 3	POSSIBILITY 4	POSSIBILITY 5	POSSIBILITY 6

RECEPTION SITE COMPARISON CHART (CONT.)

QUESTIONS	POSSIBILITY 1	POSSIBILITY 2
Are there any restrictions for rice or rose petal tossing?		
What room and table decorations are available?		
Is a changing room available?		
Is there handicap accessibility?		
Is a dance floor included in the site fee?		
Are tables, chairs, and linens included in the site fee?		
Are outside caterers allowed?		
Are kitchen facilities available for outside caterers?		
Does the facility have full liability insurance?		
What perks or giveaways are offered?		
How many parking spaces are available for my wedding party?		
How many parking spaces are available for my guests?		
What is the cost for parking, if any?		
What is the cost for sleeping rooms, if available?		
What is the payment policy?		
What is the cancellation policy?		

POSSIBILITY 3	POSSIBILITY 4	POSSIBILITY 5	POSSIBILITY 6

RECEPTION SITE INFORMATION SHEET

RECEPTION SITE:

Site Coordinator: _____ Cost: _____

Website: _____

E-mail: _____

Phone Number: _____ Fax Number: _____

Address: _____

City: _____ State: _____ Zip Code: _____

Name of Room: _____ Room Capacity: _____

Date Confirmed: _____ Confirm Head Count By: _____

Beginning Time: _____ Ending Time: _____

Cocktails/Hors d'Oeuvres Time: _____ Meal Time: _____

Color of Linens: _____ Color of Napkins: _____

Total Cost: _____

Deposit: _____ Date: _____

Balance: _____ Date Due: _____

Cancellation Policy: _____

EQUIPMENT INCLUDES:

❑ Tables   ❑ Chairs   ❑ Linens   ❑ Tableware
❑ Barware   ❑ Heaters   ❑ Electric Outlet ❑ Musical Instruments

SERVICE INCLUDES:

❑ Waiters   ❑ Bartenders   ❑ Valet   ❑ Main Meal
❑ Clean Up   ❑ Setup   ❑ Security   ❑ Free Parking

CATERER:

Contact Person: _____   Cost Per Person: _____

Website: _____

E-mail: _____

Phone Number: _____   Fax Number: _____

Address: _____

City: _____ State: _____   Zip Code: _____

Confirmed Date: _____   Confirm Head Count By: _____

Arrival Time: _____   Departure Time: _____

Cocktails/Hors d'Oeuvres Time: _____   Meal Time: _____

Color of Linens: _____   Color of Napkins: _____

Total Cost: _____

Deposit: _____ Date: _____

Balance: _____   Date Due: _____

Cancellation Policy: _____

EQUIPMENT INCLUDES:

❑ Tables   ❑ Chairs   ❑ Linens   ❑ Tableware
❑ Barware   ❑ Heaters   ❑ Lighting   ❑ Candles

SERVICE INCLUDES:

❑ Waiters   ❑ Bartenders   ❑ Setup   ❑ Clean Up
❑ Security   ❑ Hors d'Oeuvres   ❑ Buffet Meal   ❑ Seated Meal
❑ Cocktails   ❑ Champagne   ❑ Wine   ❑ Beer
❑ Punch   ❑ Soft Drinks   ❑ Coffee/Tea   ❑ Cake

TABLE SEATING ARRANGEMENTS

Complete this form only after finalizing your guest list. Make as many copies of this form as needed.

HEAD TABLE	BRIDE'S FAMILY TABLE	GROOM'S FAMILY TABLE
• TABLE __	• TABLE __	• TABLE __
• TABLE __	• TABLE __	• TABLE __

Complete this form only after finalizing your guest list. Make as many copies of this form as needed.

• TABLE __

_____
_____
_____
_____
_____
_____
_____
_____
_____

• TABLE __

_____
_____
_____
_____
_____
_____
_____
_____
_____

• TABLE __

_____
_____
_____
_____
_____
_____
_____
_____
_____

• TABLE __

_____
_____
_____
_____
_____
_____
_____
_____
_____

• TABLE __

_____
_____
_____
_____
_____
_____
_____
_____
_____

• TABLE __

_____
_____
_____
_____
_____
_____
_____
_____
_____

• TABLE __

_____
_____
_____
_____
_____
_____
_____
_____

• TABLE __

_____
_____
_____
_____
_____
_____
_____
_____

• TABLE __

_____
_____
_____
_____
_____
_____
_____
_____

LIQUOR ORDER FORM

LIQUOR STORE: _____ Date Ordered: _____

Salesperson: _____ Phone Number: _____

Website: _____

E-mail: _____

Address: _____

City: _____ State: _____ Zip Code: _____

Cost: _____

Delivered By: _____ Delivery Date: _____

TYPE OF LIQUOR: **# of Bottles Needed:**   **Price:**

_____

_____

_____

_____

_____

_____

_____

_____

_____

_____

_____

_____

_____

_____

_____

_____

TYPE OF FAVOR	Website/Company	Quantity	Price
White matchboxes engraved with names of bride and groom and date of the wedding.			
Cocktail napkins engraved with names of the bride and groom and date of the wedding.			
Almonds, chocolates, or other fine candy.			
Customized wine or champagne labels with bride and groom's names and wedding date.			
Porcelain or ceramic favors with bride and groom's names and wedding date.			
Plant or tree shoot to be planted in honor of the bride and groom.			
Other:			
Other:			
Other:			
Other:			

CATERER COMPARISON CHART

QUESTIONS	POSSIBILITY 1	POSSIBILITY 2
What is the name of the caterer?		
What is the website and e-mail of the caterer?		
What is the address of the caterer?		
What is the name and phone number of my contact person?		
How many years have you been in business?		
What percentage of your business is dedicated to receptions?		
Do you have liability insurance/license to serve alcohol?		
When is the final head-count needed?		
What is your ratio of servers to guests?		
How do your servers dress for wedding receptions?		
What is your price range for a seated lunch/buffet lunch?		
What is your price range for a seated/buffet dinner?		
How much gratuity is expected?		
What is your specialty?		
What is your cake-cutting fee?		
What is your bartending fee?		
What is your fee to clean up after the reception?		
What is your payment policy?		
What is your cancellation policy?		

POSSIBILITY 3	POSSIBILITY 4	POSSIBILITY 5	POSSIBILITY 6

MENU WORKSHEET

HORS D'OEUVRES:

_____

_____

_____

SALADS/APPETIZERS:

_____

_____

_____

SOUPS:

_____

_____

_____

MAIN ENTREE:

_____

_____

_____

DESSERTS:

_____

_____

_____

WEDDING CAKE:

_____

_____

_____

"Love is friendship set to music."
~ Anonymous

CEREMONY MUSIC 131

RECEPTION MUSIC...132

CEREMONY MUSIC COMPARISON CHART 134

RECEPTION MUSIC COMPARISON CHART 136

RECEPTION MUSIC SELECTIONS..............................138

MUSIC

PHOTO: KAREN FRENCH

MUSIC

CEREMONY MUSIC IS THE MUSIC PLAYED DURING the prelude, processional, ceremony, recessional, and postlude. Prelude music is played while guests are being seated, 15 to 30 minutes before the ceremony begins. Processional music is played as the wedding party enters the ceremony site. Recessional music is played as the wedding party leaves the ceremony site. Postlude music is played while the guests leave the ceremony site.

CEREMONY MUSIC

Options: The most traditional musical instrument for wedding ceremonies is the organ. But guitars, pianos, flutes, harps, and violins are also popular today.

Popular selections for a Christian wedding:

Trumpet Voluntary by Purcell
The Bridal Chorus by Wagner
Wedding March by Mendelssohn
Postlude in G Major by Handel
Canon in D Major by Pachelbel
Adagio in A Minor by Bach

Popular selections for a Jewish wedding:

Erev Shel Shoshanim
Erev Ba
Hana' Ava Babanot

Things to Consider: Music may or may not be included as part of the ceremony site fee. Be sure to check with your ceremony site about restrictions pertaining to music and the availability of musical instruments for your use. Discuss the selection of ceremony music with your officiant and musicians. Make sure the musicians know how to play the selections you request.

When selecting ceremony music, keep in mind the formality of your wedding, your religious affiliation, and the length of the ceremony. Also consider the location and time of day. If the ceremony is outside where there may be other noises such as traffic, wind, or people's voices, or if a large number of guests will be attending your ceremony, consider having the music, your officiant, and your vows amplified. Make sure there are electrical outlets close to where the instruments will be set up.

Tips to Save Money: Hire student musicians from your local university or high school. Ask a friend to sing or play at your ceremony; they will be honored. If you're planning to hire a band for your reception, consider hiring a scaled-down version of the same band to play at your ceremony, such as a trio of flute, guitar, and vocals. This could enable you to negotiate a "package" price. If you're planning to hire a DJ for your reception, consider hiring him/her to play pre-recorded music at your ceremony.

Price Range: $100 - $900

RECEPTION MUSIC

Music is a major part of your reception, and should be planned carefully. Music helps create the atmosphere of your wedding. Special songs will make your reception unique. When you select music for your reception, keep in mind the age and musical preference of your guests, your budget, and any restrictions that the reception site may have. Bands and musicians are typically more expensive than DJ's.

Options: There are many options for reception music: you can hire a DJ, a band, an orchestra, or any combination of one or more instruments and vocalists.

Things to Consider: Hire an entertainment agency that can help you choose a reliable DJ or band that will play the type of music you want. Whoever you choose, they should have experience performing at wedding receptions.

If you want your musician to act as a master of ceremonies, make sure s/he has a complete timeline for your reception in order to announce the various events such as the toasts, first dance, and cutting of the cake. Consider watching your musicians perform at another event before booking their services.

If you need a large variety of music to satisfy all your guests, consider hiring a DJ. A professional DJ can play any type of music and may even offer a light show. Make sure you give him/her a list of the songs you want played at your reception and the sequence in which you want them played. Make sure there are electrical outlets at the reception site close to where the musicians will be performing.

Tips to Save Money: You will probably get a better price if you hire a band or DJ directly than if you hire them through an entertainment agency. Check the music department of local colleges and universities for names of student musicians and DJs. You may be able to hire a student for a fraction of the price of a professional musician or DJ. A DJ is typically less expensive than a "live" musician. Some facilities have contracts with certain DJ's, and you may be able to save money by hiring one of them.

Price Range: $500 - $5,000

Bonus Tip: For suggestions on appropriate music for each moment of the wedding, you should consider purchasing *The Ultimate Guide to Wedding Music* from Wedding Solutions. This books contain lyrics for 100 of the most popular love songs for weddings. It also includes an audio CD with excerpts from 99 of the most popular classical music pieces for weddings.

CEREMONY MUSIC COMPARISON CHART

QUESTIONS	POSSIBILITY 1	POSSIBILITY 2
What is the name of the musician or band?		
What is the website and e-mail of the musician or band?		
What is the address of the musician or band?		
What is the name and phone number of my contact person?		
How many years of professional experience do you have?		
What percentage of your business is dedicated to weddings?		
Are you the person who will perform at my wedding?		
What instrument(s) do you play?		
What type of music do you specialize in?		
What are your hourly fees?		
What is the cost of a soloist?		
What is the cost of a duet?		
What is the cost of a trio?		
What is the cost of a quartet?		
How would you dress for my wedding?		
Do you have liability insurance?		
Do you have a cordless microphone?		
What is your payment/cancellation policy?		

CEREMONY MUSIC COMPARISON CHART

POSSIBILITY 3	POSSIBILITY 4	POSSIBILITY 5	POSSIBILITY 6

RECEPTION MUSIC COMPARISON CHART

QUESTIONS	POSSIBILITY 1	POSSIBILITY 2
What is the name of the musician? Band? DJ?		
What is the website and e-mail of the musician? Band? DJ?		
What is the address of the musician? Band? DJ?		
What is the name and phone number of my contact person?		
How many years of professional experience do you have?		
What percentage of your business is dedicated to receptions?		
How many people are in your band?		
What type of music do you specialize in?		
What type of sound system do you have?		
Can you act as a master of ceremonies? How do you dress?		
Can you provide a light show?		
Do you have a cordless microphone?		
How many breaks do you take? How long are they?		
Do you play recorded music during breaks?		
Do you have liability insurance?		
What are your fees for a 4-hour reception?		
What is your cost for each additional hour?		

POSSIBILITY 3	POSSIBILITY 4	POSSIBILITY 5	POSSIBILITY 6

RECEPTION MUSIC SELECTIONS

Make a copy of this form and give it to your musicians.

WHEN	Selection	Songwriter	Played By
Receiving Line			
During Hors d'Oeuvres			
During Dinner			
First Dance			
Second Dance			
Third Dance			
Bouquet Toss			
Garter Removal			
Cutting of the Cake			
Last Dance			
Couple Leaving			
Other:			
Other:			
Other:			
Other:			
Other:			
Other:			

"How do I love thee? Let me count the ways."
~ Elizabeth Barrett Browning

WEDDING CAKE...139

GROOM'S CAKE 140

CAKE DELIVERY/SET-UP FEE....................................140

CAKE-CUTTING FEE 140

CAKE TOP 141

CAKE KNIFE/TOASTING GLASSES 141

BAKERY COMPARISON CHART 142

BAKERY

PHOTO: KAREN FRENCH

BAKERY

WEDDING CAKES MAY BE ORDERED FROM A CATERER OR FROM A BAKERY. Some hotels and restaurants may also be able to provide a wedding cake. However, you will probably be better off ordering your cake from a bakery that specializes in wedding cakes. Ask to see photographs of other wedding cakes your baker has created, and by all means, ask for a tasting!

WEDDING CAKE

Options: When ordering your cake, you will have to decide not only on a flavor, but also on a size, shape, and color. Size is determined by the number of guests. You can choose from one large tier or more smaller tiers. The cake can be round, square, or heart-shaped. The most common flavors are chocolate, carrot, lemon, rum, and "white" cakes. You can be creative by adding a filling to your cake, such as custard, strawberry, or chocolate. You may also want to consider having tiers of different flavors.

Things to Consider: Price, workmanship, quality, and taste vary considerably from baker to baker. In addition to flavor, size, and cost, consider decoration and spoilage (sugar keeps longer than cream frostings). The cake should be beautifully displayed on its own table decorated with flowers or greenery. Make sure the baker, caterer, or reception site manager can provide you with a pretty cake-cutting knife. If not, you will need to purchase or rent one.

When determining the size of the cake, don't forget that you'll be saving the top tier for your first anniversary. This top tier should be removed before the cake is cut, wrapped in several layers of plastic wrap or put inside a plastic container, and kept frozen until your anniversary.

Tips to Save Money: Some bakers have setup and delivery fees, and some don't. Check for individuals who bake from their home. They are usually more reasonable, but you should check with your local health department before hiring one of these at-home bakers. Also, some caterers have contracts with bakeries and can pass on savings to you. Some bakeries require a deposit on columns and plates; other bakeries use disposable columns and plates, saving you the rental fee and the hassle of returning these items.

BAKERY

Price Range: $2 - $12 per piece

GROOM'S CAKE

The groom's cake is an old southern tradition whereby this cake is cut up and distributed to guests in little white boxes engraved with the bride and groom's names. Today the groom's cake, if offered, is cut and served along with the wedding cake.

Options: Usually a chocolate cake decorated with fruit.

Tips to Save Money: Because of its cost and the labor involved in cutting and distributing the cake, very few people offer this delightful custom any more.

Price Range: $1 - $2 per piece

CAKE DELIVERY/SETUP FEE

This is the fee charged by bakers to deliver and set up your wedding cake at the reception site. It usually includes a deposit on the cake pillars and plate which will be refunded upon their return to the baker.

Tips to Save Money: Have a friend or family member get a quick lesson on how to set up your cake. Have them pick it up and set it up the day of your wedding, then have the florist decorate the cake and/or cake table with flowers and greenery.

Price Range: $40 - $100

CAKE-CUTTING FEE

Most reception sites and caterers charge a fee for each slice of cake they cut if the cake is brought in from an outside bakery. This fee will probably shock you. It is simply their way of enticing you to order the cake through them. Unfortunately, many caterers will not allow a member of your party to cut the cake.

Tips to Save Money: Many hotels and restaurants include a dessert in the cost of their meal packages. If you forego this dessert and substitute your cake as the dessert, they may be willing to waive the cake-cutting fee. Be sure to ask them.

Price Range: $0.75 - $2.50 per person

CAKE TOP

The bride's cake is often topped and surrounded with fresh flowers, but traditional "cake tops" (figurines set atop the wedding cake) are also very popular.

Options: Bells, love birds, a bridal couple or replica of two wedding rings are popular choices for cake tops and can be saved as mementos of your wedding day.

Beware: Some porcelain and other heavier cake tops need to be anchored down into the cake. If you're planning to use a cake top other than flowers, be sure to discuss this with your baker.

Tips to Save Money: Borrow a cake top from a friend or a family member as "something borrowed," an age-old wedding tradition (see page 236).

Price Range: $20 - $150

CAKE KNIFE/TOASTING GLASSES

Your cake knife and toasting glasses should complement your overall setting; these items will bring you happy memories of your wedding day every time you use them. The cake knife is used to cut the cake at the reception. The bride usually cuts the first two slices of the wedding cake with the groom's hand placed over hers. The groom feeds the bride first. Then the bride feeds the groom. This tradition makes beautiful wedding photographs.

You will need toasting glasses to toast each other after cutting the cake. They are usually decorated with ribbons or flowers and kept near the cake. This tradition also makes beautiful wedding photographs.

Things to Consider: Consider having your initials and wedding date engraved on your wedding knife as a memento. Consider purchasing crystal or silver toasting glasses as a keepsake of your wedding. Have your florist decorate your knife and toasting glasses with flowers or ribbons.

Tips to Save Money: Borrow your cake knife or toasting glasses from a friend or family member as "something borrowed," an age-old wedding tradition (see page 236). Use the reception facility's glasses and knife, and decorate them with flowers or ribbon.

Price Range: $15 - $120 for knife; $10 - $100 for toasting glasses

BAKERY COMPARISON CHART

QUESTIONS	POSSIBILITY 1	POSSIBILITY 2
What is the name of the bakery?		
What is the bakery's website and e-mail?		
What is the address of the bakery?		
What is the name and phone number of my contact person?		
How many years have you been making wedding cakes?		
What are your wedding cake specialties?		
Do you offer free tasting of your wedding cakes?		
Are your wedding cakes fresh or frozen?		
How far in advance should I order my cake?		
Can you make a groom's cake?		
Do you lend, rent, or sell cake knives?		
What is the cost per serving of my desired cake?		
What is your cake pillar and plate rental fee, if any?		
Is this fee refundable upon the return of these items?		
When must these items be returned?		
What is your cake delivery and setup fee?		
What is your payment policy?		
What is your cancellation policy?		

POSSIBILITY 3	POSSIBILITY 4	POSSIBILITY 5	POSSIBILITY 6

NOTES

"Life is the flower for which love is the honey."
~ Victor Hugo

BRIDE'S BOUQUET..145

TOSSING BOUQUET..147

MAID OF HONOR'S & BRIDESMAIDS' BOUQUETS.........147

MAID OF HONOR'S & BRIDESMAIDS' HAIRPIECE 148

FLOWER GIRL'S HAIRPIECE.......................................148

BRIDE'S GOING AWAY CORSAGE 148

FAMILY MEMBERS' CORSAGES....................................149

GROOM'S BOUTONNIERE..149

USHERS/OTHER FAMILY MEMBERS' BOUTONNIERES....150

MAIN ALTAR 150

ALTAR CANDELABRA, AISLE PEWS 151

RECEPTION SITE, HEAD TABLE, GUEST TABLES 152

BUFFET TABLE, PUNCH TABLE, CAKE TABLE 153

CAKE, CAKE KNIFE, TOASTING GLASSES 154

FLORAL DELIVERY/SET UP...154

FLORIST COMPARISON CHART 156

BOUQUETS AND FLOWERS...158

FLOWERS AND THEIR SEASONS..................................161

POPULAR WEDDING FLOWERS 163

PHOTOS OF POPULAR WEDDING FLOWERS.................183

PHOTO: KAREN FRENCH

FLOWERS

Groom

FLOWERS

FLOWERS ADD BEAUTY, FRAGRANCE, AND COLOR TO YOUR WEDDING. Like everything else, flowers should fit your overall style and color scheme. The purpose of flowers at the main altar is to direct the guests' visual attention toward the front of the church and to the bridal couple. Therefore, they must be seen by guests seated toward the back. You may also want to use flowers or ribbons to mark the aisle pews and add color.

BRIDE'S BOUQUET

The bridal bouquet is one of the most important elements of the bride's attire and deserves special attention. Start by selecting the color and shape of the bouquet. The bridal bouquet should be carried low enough so that all the intricate details of your gown are visible.

Options: There are many colors, scents, sizes, shapes, and styles of bouquets to choose from. Popular styles are the cascade, cluster, contemporary, and hand-tied garden bouquets. The traditional bridal bouquet is made of white flowers. Stephanotis, gardenias, white roses, orchids, and lilies of the valley are popular choices for an all-white bouquet.

If you prefer a colorful bouquet, you may want to consider using roses, tulips, stock, peonies, freesia, and gerbera, which come in a wide variety of colors. Using scented flowers in your bouquet will evoke memories of your wedding day whenever you smell them in the future. Popular fragrant flowers are gardenias, freesia, stephanotis, bouvardia, and narcissus. Select flowers that are in season to assure availability (see pages 163-192).

Things to Consider: Your flowers should complement the season, your gown, your color scheme, your attendants' attire, and the style and formality of your wedding. If you have a favorite flower, build your bouquet around it and include it in all your arrangements. Some flowers carry centuries of symbolism. Consider stephanotis—tradition regards it as the bridal good-luck flower! Pimpernel signifies change; white flowers radiate innocence; forget-me-nots indicate true love; and ivy stands for friendship, fidelity, and matrimony—the three essentials for a happy marriage.

FLOWERS

No flower, however, has as much symbolism for brides as the orange blossom, having at least 700 years of nuptial history. Its unusual ability to simultaneously bear flowers and produce fruit symbolizes the fusion of beauty, personality, and fertility.

Whatever flowers you select, final arrangements should be made well in advance of your wedding date to insure availability. Confirm your final order and delivery time a few days before the wedding. Have the flowers delivered before the photographer arrives so that you can include them in your pre-ceremony photos.

In determining the size of your bouquet, consider your gown and your overall stature. Carry a smaller bouquet if you're petite or if your gown is fairly ornate. A long, cascading bouquet complements a fairly simple gown or a tall or larger bride. Arm bouquets look best when resting naturally in the crook of your arm.

For a natural, fresh-picked look, have your florist put together a cluster of flowers tied together with a ribbon. For a Victorian appeal, carry a nosegay or a basket filled with flowers. Or carry a Bible or other family heirloom decorated with just a few flowers. For a contemporary look, you may want to consider carrying an arrangement of calla lilies or other long-stemmed flower over your arm. For a dramatic statement, carry a single stem of your favorite flower!

Beware: If your bouquet includes delicate flowers that will not withstand hours of heat or a lack of water, make sure your florist uses a bouquet holder to keep them fresh. If you want to carry fresh-cut stems without a bouquet holder, make sure the flowers you select are hardy enough to go without water for the duration of your ceremony and reception.

Tips to Save Money: The cost of some flowers may be significantly higher during their off season. Try to select flowers that are in bloom and plentiful at the time of your wedding. Avoid exotic, out-of-season flowers. Allow your florist to emphasize your colors using more reasonable, seasonal flowers to achieve your overall look. If you have a favorite flower that is costly or out of season, consider using silk for that one flower.

Avoid scheduling your wedding on holidays such as Valentine's Day and Mother's Day when the price of flowers is higher. Because every attendant will carry or wear flowers, consider keeping the size of your wedding party down to accommodate your floral budget.

Price Range: $75 - $400

TOSSING BOUQUET

If you want to preserve your bridal bouquet, consider having your florist make a smaller, less expensive bouquet specifically for tossing. This will be the bouquet you toss to your single, female friends toward the end of the reception. Tradition has it that the woman who catches the bouquet is the next to be married. Have your florist include a few sprigs of fresh ivy in the tossing bouquet to symbolize friendship and fidelity.

Tips to Save Money: Use the floral cake top or guest book table "tickler bouquet" as the tossing bouquet. Or omit the tossing bouquet altogether and simply toss your bridal bouquet.

Price Range: $20 - $100

MAID OF HONOR'S BOUQUET

The maid of honor's bouquet can be somewhat larger or of a different color than the rest of the bridesmaids' bouquets. This will help to set her apart from the others.

Price Range: $25 - $100

BRIDESMAIDS' BOUQUETS

The bridesmaids' bouquets should complement the bridal bouquet, but are generally smaller in size. The size and color should coordinate with the bridesmaids' dresses and the overall style of the wedding. Bridesmaids' bouquets are usually identical.

Options: To personalize your bridesmaids' bouquets, insert a different flower in each of their bouquets to make a statement. For example, if one of your bridesmaids has been sad, give her a lily of the valley to symbolize the return of happiness. To tell a friend that you admire her, insert yellow jasmine. A pansy will let your friend know that you are thinking of her.

Things to Consider: Choose a bouquet style (cascade, cluster, contemporary, hand-tied) that complements the formality of your wedding and the height of your attendants. If your bridesmaids will be wearing floral print dresses, select flowers that complement the floral print.

Tips to Save Money: Have your attendants carry a single stemmed rose, lily, or other suitable flower for an elegant look that also saves money.

Price Range: $25 - $100

FLOWERS

MAID OF HONOR/BRIDESMAIDS' HAIRPIECE

For a garden look, have your maid of honor and bridesmaids wear garlands of flowers in their hair. If so, provide your maid of honor with a slightly different color or variety of flower to set her apart from the others.

Options: You may consider using artificial flowers for the hairpieces as long as they are in keeping with the flowers carried by members of the bridal party. Since it is not always easy to find good artificial blooms, other types of hairpieces may be more satisfactory, durable, and attractive.

Things to Consider: Flowers used for the hairpiece must be a sturdy and long-lived variety.

Price Range: $8 - $100

FLOWER GIRL'S HAIRPIECE

Flower girls often wear a wreath of flowers as a hairpiece.

Options: This is another place where artificial flowers may be used, but they must be in keeping with the flowers carried by members of the bridal party. Since it is not always easy to find good artificial blooms, other types of hairpieces may be more satisfactory, durable, and attractive.

Things to Consider: If the flowers used for the hairpiece are not a sturdy and long-lived variety, a ribbon, bow, or hat might be a safer choice.

Price Range: $8 - $75

BRIDE'S GOING AWAY CORSAGE

You may want to consider wearing a corsage on your going away outfit. This makes for pretty photos as you and your new husband leave the reception for your honeymoon. Have your florist create a corsage which echoes the beauty of your bouquet.

Beware: Put a protective shield under lilies when using them as a corsage, as their anthers will easily stain fabric. Be careful when using alstroemeria as a corsage, as its sap can be harmful if it enters the human bloodstream.

Tips to Save Money: Ask your florist if s/he can design your bridal bouquet in such a way that the center flowers may be removed and worn as a corsage. Or omit this corsage altogether.

Price Range: $10 - $50

FAMILY MEMBERS' CORSAGES

The groom is responsible for providing flowers for his mother, the bride's mother, and the grandmothers. The officiant, if female, may also be given a corsage to reflect her important role in the ceremony. The corsages don't have to be identical, but they should be coordinated with the color of their dresses.

Options: The groom may order flowers that can be pinned to a pocketbook or worn around a wrist. He should ask which style the women prefer, and if a particular color is needed to coordinate with their dresses. Gardenias, camellias, white orchids, or cymbidium orchids are excellent choices for corsages, as they go well with any outfit.

Things to Consider: The groom may also want to consider ordering corsages for other close family members, such as sisters and aunts. This will add a little to your floral expenses but will make these female family members feel more included in your wedding and will let guests know that they are related to the bride and groom. Many women do not like to wear corsages, so the groom should check with the people involved before ordering the flowers.

Beware: Put a protective shield under lilies when using them as corsages, as their anthers will easily stain fabric. Be careful when using alstroemeria as corsages, as its sap can be harmful if it enters the human bloodstream.

Tips to Save Money: Ask your florist to recommend reasonable flowers for corsages. Dendrobium orchids are reasonable and make lovely corsages.

Price Range: $10 - $35

GROOM'S BOUTONNIERE

The groom wears his boutonniere on the left lapel, nearest to his heart.

Options: Boutonnieres are generally a single blossom such as a rosebud, stephanotis, freesia, or a miniature carnation. If a rosebud is used for the wedding party, have the groom wear two rosebuds, or add a sprig of baby's breath to differentiate him from the groomsmen.

Things to Consider: You may use a small cluster of flowers instead of a single bloom for the groom's boutonniere.

Beware: Be careful when using alstroemeria as a boutonniere, as its sap can be harmful if it enters the human bloodstream.

Tips to Save Money: Use mini-carnations rather than roses.

Price Range: $4 - $25

USHERS/OTHER FAMILY MEMBERS' BOUTONNIERES

The groom gives each man in his wedding party a boutonniere to wear on his left lapel. The officiant, if male, may also be given a boutonniere to reflect his important role in the ceremony. The ring bearer may or may not wear a boutonniere, depending on his outfit. A boutonniere is more appropriate on a tuxedo than on knickers and knee socks.

Options: Generally, a single blossom such as a rosebud, freesia, or miniature carnation is used as a boutonniere.

Things to Consider: The groom should also consider ordering boutonnieres for other close family members such as fathers, grandfathers, and brothers. This will add a little to your floral expenses, but will make these male family members feel more included in your wedding and will let guests know that they are related to the bride and groom.

Beware: Be careful when using alstroemeria as boutonnieres, as its sap can be harmful if it enters the human bloodstream.

Tips to Save Money: Use mini-carnations rather than roses.

Price Range: $3 - $15

MAIN ALTAR

The purpose of flowers at the main altar is to direct the guests' visual attention toward the front of the church or synagogue and to the bridal couple. Therefore, they must be seen by guests seated in the back. The flowers for the ceremony site can be as elaborate or as simple as you wish. Your officiant's advice, or that of the altar guild or florist, can be most helpful in choosing flowers for the altar and chancel.

Options: If your ceremony is outside, decorate the arch, gazebo, or other structure serving as the altar with flowers or greenery. In a Jewish ceremony, vows are said under a Chuppah, which is placed at the altar and covered with greens and fresh flowers.

Things to Consider: In choosing floral accents, consider the decor of your ceremony site. Some churches and synagogues are ornate enough and don't need extra flowers. Too many arrangements would get lost in the architectural splendor. Select a few dramatic showpieces that will complement the existing decor. Be sure to ask if there are any restrictions on flowers at the church or synagogue. Remember, decorations should be determined by the size and style of the building, the formality of the wedding, the preferences of the bride, the cost, and the regulations of the particular site.

Tips to Save Money: Decorate the ceremony site with greenery only. Candlelight and greenery are elegant in and of themselves. Use greenery and flowers from your garden. Have your ceremony outside in a beautiful garden or by the water, surrounded by nature's own splendor.

Price Range: $50 - $3,000

ALTAR CANDELABRA

In a candlelight ceremony, the candelabra may be decorated with flowers or greens for a dramatic effect.

Options: Ivy may be twined around the candelabra, or flowers may be strung to them.

Price Range: $50 - $200

AISLE PEWS

Flowers, candles, or ribbons are often used to mark the aisle pews and add color.

Options: A cluster of flowers, a cascade of greens, or a cascade of flowers and ribbons are all popular choices. Candles with adorning greenery add an elegant touch.

Things to Consider: Use hardy flowers that can tolerate being handled as pew ornaments. Gardenias and camellias, for example, are too sensitive to last long.

Beware: Avoid using allium in your aisle pew decorations as they have an odor of onions.

Tips to Save Money: It is not necessary to decorate all of the aisle pews, or any at all. To save money, decorate only the reserved family pews. Or decorate every second or third pew.

Price Range: $5 - $75

FLOWERS

RECEPTION SITE

Flowers add beauty, fragrance, and color to your reception. Flowers for the reception, like everything else, should fit your overall style and color scheme. Flowers can help transform a stark reception hall into a warm, inviting, and colorful room.

Things to Consider: You can rent indoor plants or small trees to give your reception a garden-like atmosphere. Decorate them with twinkle lights to achieve a magical effect.

Tips to Save Money: You can save money by taking flowers from the ceremony to the reception site for decorations. However, you must coordinate this move carefully to avoid having your guests arrive at an undecorated reception room. Use greenery rather than flowers to fill large areas. Trees and garlands of ivy can give a dramatic impact for little money. Use greenery and flowers from your garden. Have your reception outside in a beautiful garden or by the water, surrounded by nature's own beauty.

Price Range: $300 - $3,000

HEAD TABLE

The head table is where the wedding party will sit during the reception. This important table should be decorated with a larger or more dramatic centerpiece than the guest tables.

Things to Consider: Consider using a different color or style of arrangement to set the head table apart from the other tables.

Beware: Avoid using highly fragrant flowers, such as narcissus, on tables where food is being served or eaten, as their fragrance may conflict with other aromas.

Tips to Save Money: Decorate the head table with the bridal and attendants' bouquets.

Price Range: $100 - $600

GUEST TABLES

At a reception where guests are seated, a small flower arrangement may be placed on each table.

Things to Consider: The arrangements should complement the table linens and the size of the table, and should be kept low enough so as not to hinder conversation among guests seated across from each other.

Beware: Avoid using highly fragrant flowers, like narcissus, on tables where food is being served or eaten, as their fragrance may conflict with other aromas.

Tips to Save Money: To keep the cost down and for less formal receptions, use small potted flowering plants placed in white baskets, or consider using dried or silk arrangements that you can make yourself and give later as gifts. Or place a wreath of greenery entwined with colored ribbon in the center of each table. Use a different colored ribbon at each table and assign your guests to tables by ribbon color instead of number.

Price Range: $10 - $100

BUFFET TABLE

If buffet tables are used, have some type of floral arrangement on the tables to add color and beauty to your display of food.

Options: Whole fruits and bunches of berries offer a variety of design possibilities. Figs add a festive touch. Pineapples are a sign of hospitality. Vegetables offer an endless array of options to decorate with. Herbs are yet another option in decorating. A mixture of rosemary and mint combined with scented geraniums makes a very unique table decoration.

Things to Consider: Depending on the size of the table, place one or two arrangements at each side.

Beware: Avoid placing certain flowers, such as carnations, snapdragons, or the star of Bethlehem, next to buffet displays of fruits or vegetables, as they are extremely sensitive to the gasses emitted by these foods.

Price Range: $50 - $500

PUNCH TABLE

Put an assortment of greens or a small arrangement of flowers at the punch table. See "Buffet Table."

Price Range: $10 - $100

CAKE TABLE

The wedding cake is often the central location at the reception. Decorate the cake table with flowers.

Tips to Save Money: Have your bridesmaids place their bouquets on the cake table during the reception, or decorate the cake top only and surround the base with greenery and a few loose flowers.

Price Range: $30 - $300

FLOWERS

CAKE

Flowers are a beautiful addition to a wedding cake and are commonly seen spilling out between the cake tiers.

Things to Consider: Use only nonpoisonous flowers, and have your florist—not the caterer—design the floral decorations for your cake. A florist will be able to blend the cake decorations into your overall floral theme.

Price Range: $20 - $100

CAKE KNIFE

Decorate your cake knife with a white satin ribbon and flowers.

Things to Consider: Consider engraving the cake knife with your names and wedding date.

Price Range: $5 - $35

TOASTING GLASSES

Tie small flowers with white ribbon onto the stems of your champagne glasses. These wedding accessories deserve a special floral touch since they will most likely be included in your special photographs.

Things to Consider: Consider engraving your toasting glasses with your names and wedding date.

Price Range: $10 - $35

FLORAL DELIVERY/SETUP

Most florists charge a fee to deliver flowers to the ceremony and reception sites and to arrange them on site.

Things to Consider: Make sure your florist knows where your sites are and what time to arrive for setup.

Price Range: $25 - $200

FLORIST COMPARISON CHART

QUESTIONS	POSSIBILITY 1	POSSIBILITY 2
What is the name of the florist?		
What is the website and e-mail of the florist?		
What is the address of the florist?		
What are your business hours?		
What is the name and phone number of my contact person?		
How many years of professional floral experience do you have?		
What percentage of your business is dedicated to weddings?		
Do you have access to out-of-season flowers?		
Will you visit my wedding sites to make floral recommendations?		
Can you preserve my bridal bouquet?		
Do you rent vases and candleholders?		
Can you provide silk flowers?		
What is the cost of the desired bridal bouquet?		
What is the cost of the desired boutonniere?		
What is the cost of the desired corsage?		
Do you have liability insurance?		
What are your delivery/setup fees?		
What is your payment/cancellation policy?		

POSSIBILITY 3	POSSIBILITY 4	POSSIBILITY 5	POSSIBILITY 6

BOUQUETS AND FLOWERS

BRIDE'S BOUQUET

Color Scheme: _____

Style: _____

Flowers: _____

_____

_____

Greenery: _____

Other (Ribbons, etc.): _____

MAID OF HONOR'S BOUQUET

Color Scheme: _____

Style: _____

Flowers: _____

_____

_____

Greenery: _____

Other (Ribbons, etc.): _____

BRIDESMAIDS' BOUQUETS

Color Scheme: _____

Style: _____

Flowers: _____

_____

_____

Greenery: _____

Other (Ribbons, etc.): _____

FLOWER GIRL'S BOUQUET

Color Scheme:

Style:

Flowers:

Greenery:

Other (Ribbons, etc.):

OTHER

Groom's Boutonniere:

Ushers' and Other Family Members' Boutonnieres:

Mother of the Bride Corsage:

Mother of the Groom Corsage:

Altar or Chuppah:

Steps to Altar or Chuppah:

BOUQUETS AND FLOWERS

OTHER

Pews: _____

_____

Entrance to the Ceremony: _____

_____

Entrance to the Reception: _____

_____

Receiving Line: _____

_____

Head Table: _____

_____

Parents' Table: _____

_____

Guest Table: _____

_____

Cake Table: _____

_____

Serving Table (Buffet, Dessert): _____

_____

Gift Table: _____

_____

FLOWER	Winter	Spring	Summer	Fall
Allium		X	X	
Alstroemeria	X	X	X	X
Amaryllis	X		X	
Anemone	X	X		X
Aster	X	X	X	X
Baby's Breath	X	X	X	X
Bachelor's Button	X	X	X	X
Billy Buttons		X	X	
Bird of Paradise	X	X	X	X
Bouvardia	X	X	X	X
Calla Lily	X	X	X	X
Carnation	X	X	X	X
Celosia		X	X	
Chrysanthemum	X	X	X	X
Daffodils		X		
Dahlia			X	X
Delphinium			X	X
Eucalyptus	X	X	X	X
Freesia	X	X	X	X
Gardenia	X	X	X	X
Gerbera	X	X	X	X
Gladiolus	X	X	X	X
Iris	X	X	X	X
Liatris	X	X	X	X
Lily	X	X	X	X

FLOWER	Winter	Spring	Summer	Fall
Lily of the Valley		X		
Lisianthus		X	X	X
Narcissus	X	X		X
Nerine	X	X	X	X
Orchid (Cattleya)	X	X	X	X
Orchid (Cymbidium)	X	X	X	X
Peony		X		
Pincushion			X	
Protea	X			X
Queen Anne's Lace			X	
Ranunculas		X		
Rose	X	X	X	X
Saponaria			X	
Snapdragon		X	X	X
Speedwell			X	
Star of Bethlehem	X			X
Statice	X	X	X	X
Stephanotis	X	X	X	X
Stock	X	X	X	X
Sunflower		X	X	X
Sweet Pea		X		
Tuberose			X	X
Tulip	X	X		
Waxflower	X	X		

POPULAR WEDDING FLOWERS

THIS SECTION CONTAINS INFORMATION ON the most popular flowers used in weddings. Each floral description is listed alphabetically by the flower's most commonly used name and includes the flower's historical significance in weddings, its main usage, proper care, durability, things to beware of, and much more. We hope this section gives you a better understanding of flowers and helps you make the appropriate floral selections for your wedding.

ALLIUM

There are two types of allium: the giant allium and the miniature allium. The giant variety is a fluffy, bubble-shaped purple flower which is 4-10 inches in diameter and sits on a stem that is at least two feet long. The smaller allium is egg-shaped with flowers that are only 1-2 inches across and sit atop a stem that is half the size of its giant brother.

These flowers, which come from the mountains in ancient China, are excellent for banquet table arrangements because of their striking appearance. Although, it is best to use these flowers on a table from which you are offering food such as hors d'oeuvres, because they do have an odor of onions. But if you place these flowers in water 24 hours before the wedding, much of the odor will be eliminated.

Historically, these flowers are used at weddings because onions were a sign of good luck and health. The smaller varieties are available throughout most of the year, but the giant allium are only available in the late spring and early summer. They will keep for about ten days.

ALSTROEMERIA

Native to South America, alstroemeria is named for the Swedish jurist Clas Alstroemer. This automatically makes the flower appropriate for weddings since marriage is an official act.

POPULAR WEDDING FLOWERS

Also known as a Peruvian lily, there are more than 50 varieties within the alstroemeria assortment in popular colors and shades. Alstroemeria are available all year in hues of pink, salmon, orange, red, lavender, and yellow. During the winter, spring and fall, they may be purchased in white. The whitest varieties currently available are "Bianca," "Paloma" and "Casablanca." The orchid-like "Casablanca" has large, beautiful white flowers with less striping on the petals.

The flowers typically are multicolored clusters on a stalk. They are excellent and economical for wedding table arrangements because one stem contains many clusters, which makes the table arrangement look like it contains lots of flowers. The alstroemeria's worldwide popularity is attributed to its versatility and long life. It is ideal for use in mixed bouquets, arrangements, corsages, on its own or by the bunch in a vase. With proper care, alstroemeria will last 2-3 weeks. A word of warning: Alstroemeria contains a chemical that may cause dermatitis in susceptible people, and sap from the alstroemeria can be harmful if it enters the human bloodstream. So handle these cut flowers with care!

AMARYLLIS

Amaryllis, botanically known as Hippeastrum, is sometimes called the belladonna lily. It is a bulb flower which originated in South Africa. Its unusual star-shaped flowers sit majestically atop a large, hollow stem. Shaded in colors of crimson, pink and white, this flower makes an excellent focal point for a table arrangement or an altar arrangement. Amaryllis first becomes available in the late summer and is readily available until year's end. The flower is odorless. If you are getting married at Christmas time, we recommend using a few "Christmas Gift" white amaryllis within your flower decor. The flower will remain open for five days.

ANEMONES

The anemone has many names in many different parts of the country. It is sometimes called a windflower, sometimes a poppy, and also a lily of the field. The anemone was first discovered in China in the early 1900s by Italian explorers who brought the flower back with them because they were so impressed by its texture and regal coloration. In Italy these flowers were made into a crown and worn by the bride at weddings.

The anemone's vibrant purple, pink, red, blue and white flowers often come with a contrasting center. They stand on a long, bending stem, which makes them useful in hair ornaments.

The average anemone will keep for a week. It has no scent. A word of caution: do not mix this flower with narcissus; the anemone is sensitive to the gasses emitted from the narcissus stem.

ASTERS

The aster is a long-lasting perennial with American roots. It was first discovered by the early settlers and was originally called "the ancestor flower." It acquired this name because it was passed along from one generation to another. This gives its place at a wedding particular significance as family members witness a major step in their next generation.

The white "Monte Cassino" aster is a bushy, double-flower variety with a diameter of 2-4 inches. There are also single-flowered varieties, notably the "Pink Star," "Blue Star," and "White Star," which are becoming increasingly popular. These flowers are generally available all year and are excellent in both bouquets and table arrangements to add fullness to the design. One of the sparser varieties is the "Climax," which is available only in late September and October. Asters will frequently last up to one week after the wedding.

BABY'S BREATH

Baby's breath is botanically named Gypsophila and contains hundreds of tiny white or pink flowers covering a multitude of intertwining stems. This wonderful filler flower is perfect as a backdrop to any arrangement or bouquet. Because the flowers are less than 1/4 inch in diameter, they set off the top note flower in a bridal bouquet. It is also possible to dye them other colors to match your wedding decor without harming them. Baby's breath, sometimes referred to as "gyp," is available year-round.

Baby's breath is an excellent flower to use at weddings because Gypsophila is derived from the Greek word Philein which means "to love." The plant was first discovered in the Mediterranean. Shortly thereafter, species were discovered as far away as Siberia. The Dutch and Israelis have been growing this long-lasting flower for the last 200 years. It has a life span of up to three weeks and has no scent.

BACHELOR'S BUTTON

What more appropriate flower for a wedding than a Bachelor's Button? Botanically it is called Centaurea. It is one of the rare, strikingly blue flowers. It is appropriately used at weddings since the groom is no longer a bachelor and no longer blue. Ushers frequently wear this flower in their lapels.

In many parts of the U.S. this flower is more commonly known as a cornflower, so called because it was originally a weed found in cornfields. The flower has been actively grown as a commercial product since the mid-1400s. Lately the Dutch have produced different colors of this two inch diameter flower. You can purchase the variety in pure white, scarlet, and pink from early spring into early winter. The normal keeping period of a Bachelor's Button is about five days.

POPULAR WEDDING FLOWERS

BILLY BUTTONS

Craspedia globosa originated in the Outback of Australia. Its common name is "drumsticks," but native Aussies gave it the nickname Billy Buttons.

The Billy Button is a globular flower which grows atop an unbranched and leafless stem. The stems are approximately six inches long, and its pom-pom like flower gives it the look of the drumstick used to beat a bass drum.

The flowers are yellow and are used to add interest to a table arrangement. If properly cared for, they will last up to two weeks.

BIRD OF PARADISE

The bird of paradise is the common name for Strelitzia. The flower was named after King George III of England's wife, Charlotte von Mecklenburg-Strelitz. The royal lady was admired for her elegance and color, so it was most appropriate that this elegant, colorful flower be named in her honor. Strelitzia originated in South Africa.

The flower sits atop a three-foot stalk. It is two-toned: orange and blue. It received its common bird of paradise name because it actually gives the appearance of a beautiful bird perched on a stalk.

Available year-round, the bird of paradise is used primarily at weddings to project a note of elegance in table decorations. It is best to use this unscented flower sparingly in floral design so as not to detract from its impact. It will last about two weeks.

BOUVARDIA

A fragrant bloom often used for weddings, Bouvardia seems to have everything going for it. It has a characteristic scent, making it especially appealing for bouquet work and small arrangements. It has an incredibly long vase life of three weeks and is available year-round.

The flowers are delicate and grow in clusters. Each tubular Bouvardia blossom is star shaped. The flower is formed by a cluster of these regularly shaped stars and is set off by simple leaves, which make an excellent frame for the blossoms. Each flower in the cluster is about one inch in diameter. The Bouvardia blossom comes in shades of white, pink, salmon and red.

Historically, the Bouvardia was known for its curative abilities. It was named in honor of Dr. Charles Bouvard, who was the physician to King Louis XII. He created hundreds of different medicines using the flower. The King thought this flower was responsible for his long life. Symbolically, Bouvardia is welcome at weddings as brides and grooms are toasted for a long life. This extremely fragrant variety will last in excess of two weeks.

CALLA LILY

Although the calla lily isn't really a lily, it shares many of the lily's qualities. It first became popular in the U.S. when Katherine Hepburn said, "The calla lilies are in bloom again ..." in *Stage Door*. The elegant Ms. Hepburn has long been associated with this traditional, long-lasting and elegant flower, which is grown primarily in England and Holland.

Calla lilies, botanically named Zantedeschia, are named after Italian botanist Zantedeschi, who discovered them in South Africa. They were given the name "calla" from the Greek word "kallos," meaning beautiful.

Sitting regally above its 2- to 3-foot stalk, the Calla is an extremely decorative flower. With a trumpet-like shape that captivates the eye, it is frequently used in wedding receptions and at the church to herald the bride.

Calla lilies are available year-round in white, yellow, red and pink coloration. Although they are dominating in appearance, their scent is insignificant.

CARNATIONS

Even the most demanding bride will be satisfied by the vast selection of carnations available. No other flower offers a better selection of colors, shades and types. The botanical name for carnation is Dianthus. Appropriately, this name translates from the Greek as "divine flower." It is the perfect flower for such a divine event as a wedding ceremony or reception. Available year-round in every size, from standard to giant to mini-spray carnations, they are extremely popular. First discovered on the west coast of Europe, carnations truly bloomed as a favorite when they were brought to America in the early 1900s. Fascinated by its exceedingly large variety, Americans adopted the flower as their own, and Europeans soon began referring to it as the "American carnation."

Through breeding techniques, the variations of this sweet smelling flower were so great that their numbers swelled by the dozens each year. Available in either full-size or miniature varieties, carnations are grown in large numbers in California, Holland and South America and are available year-round. Because of their abundance, except for rare varieties, they will be affordable on any wedding budget. Each stem contains multiple flowers, which makes them even more attractive from an economic as well as a visual standpoint. Carnations are commonly used to frame the walkway in the church, as a bridal canopy, as boutonnieres, and in floral arrangements. One note of caution: avoid placing carnation arrangements next to buffet displays of fruit or vegetables as the flower is quite sensitive to the gasses they emit.

POPULAR WEDDING FLOWERS

CHRYSANTHEMUM

The chrysanthemum, or mum, is one of the most abundant and popular flowers in the world. One can trace its origin to the western part of Russia. The botanical and the common name are identical and come from the Latin word meaning "yellow flower." Although yellow is the most common color, they are available in many other colors as well as color combinations. The giant version of the flower is also referred to as a Pom-Pom and is the flower of choice at football games.

Available year-round in a multitude of shapes and sizes, the chrysanthemum is a preferred flower at weddings. A white variety, the "Marguerite," was used by French, Italian and English royalty at weddings to signify that the choice of bride by the groom was purely correct. In the U.S., two varieties the "Happy" and the "Funshine," are frequently chosen for table decorations and wedding aisle arrangements.

The shapes of the mum include puffball, daisy-like, tubular, and spider-like varieties. Even though many different colored mums can be obtained from a florist, the hearty nature of the chrysanthemum makes it possible for the flowers to be successfully dyed to match a particular wedding color scheme. Except for mums that are dyed, arrangements usually last 2-3 weeks after the final toast to the bride and groom.

CELOSIA

The celosia is known by many names in many lands. It is sometimes called a crested cockscomb; sometimes a burnt plume; a plume celosia; a chinese wool flower or a plumed brain flower ... the latter because its ruffled flowers resemble the focal point of the mind. This flower was first used at weddings to symbolize the joining of one's mind to one's mate.

The foliage comes in deep shades of orange, red, yellow, purple and creamy white. The flame varieties appear as compact spikes, while the cockscomb varieties have compact heads like the comb on a rooster's head. The coarse flowers sit atop a thick, fleshy stalk and become the focal point of any arrangement in which they are included. The heads of the flowers are 2-8 inches across and, when cut to size, make an exciting and attractive decoration for the bride and groom's place setting. After the wedding, they can easily be dried and kept as a remembrance.

These flowers first originated in Africa, but the first known cultivated varieties came from Japan. They are available from May until September. They have no scent and are best used at indoor functions since they have a tendency to react to atmospheric differences and spot easily.

DAFFODIL

The daffodil, although common, is unusual in that its common name and its scientific name, narcissus, are equally well known by the general public. Legend has it that the name of the flower comes from a youth who was so in love with his own beauty that the gods turned him into this beautiful narcissus flower. To this day, self love is still referred to by the term "narcissistic." You can find daffodils in white, pink, and multicolored varieties. The majority, however, are yellow.

The flower is trumpet shaped with star-like petals projecting from the center. Its leaves are strap-shaped. You are best off getting your daffodils from a greenhouse. An easy way to tell if your daffodils are from a greenhouse is that greenhouse grown narcissus are generally delivered with their leaves, while the field grown flowers are typically delivered without their leaves.

In planning wedding arrangements, remember that this flower is quite fragrant, so make sure it is placed in areas where it will not conflict with other aromas. The "Paper white" variety is very attractive, but be aware that this particular variety has an extremely pungent odor. Another word of caution: the stems tend to get slimy in water, but this can easily be counteracted with preservative. Daffodils generally last more than a week. Although some varieties are available between November and April, keep in mind that this sunny yellow bulb flower is least expensive during its growing season in the spring.

DAHLIA

The dahlia was first discovered in the plains of Mexico nearly 400 years ago, where it was called acoctli. Although quite beautiful in appearance, nothing was done to bring about its cultivation until 200 years later. At that time, botanical experts in Mexico sent a gift of dahlia seeds to the royal gardens in Madrid, where they were cultivated and given as a gift to the wife of the Mexican ambassador to the Spanish court.

The flower was named in honor of a noted botanical author from Sweden, A. Dahl. Dahlias immediately became popular for use in royal functions, and members of the royal court sought them out to establish their position in society.

Dahlias have a strong, spicy smell and are available in a broad range of shapes, from fluffy to cactus to pom-pom to peony flower. Most of the dahlias today are cultivated in Holland, but Californians have recently become more interested in developing hybrids. Dahlias are increasingly available from July through November.

Dahlias come in a variety of colors that include purple, lavender, red, yellow, pink and even bronze and white. The newest varieties include two-tone flowers. Dahlias measure 4-8 inches across and sit on stems that are 1-3 feet in length. When the dahlia is in full bloom, it makes an excellent decorative hair piece or bridal bouquet adornment. Its average vase life is 1-2 weeks. These flowers are similar in appearance to chrysanthemums and, when feasible, may be used in their place in arrangements.

POPULAR WEDDING FLOWERS

DELPHINIUM

A summer wedding is the perfect time to feature delphinium. Although most varieties are available year-round, all varieties are readily available from June through November. Also known as larkspur, this multi-bloomed flower is regal yet soft in appearance. It has spike-shaped flower clusters of disc-shaped flowers that are 1-2 inches. They tower in 8- to 10-inch spikes on stems 1 1/2 - 4 feet long. Useful alone in vases or for decoration, they will last at least one week. They are popularly used in Flemish-style bouquets.

A perfect variety for an "old fashioned wedding" theme, delphinium originated in Asia, although today they can be found in cultivation on most continents. Delphinium consolida was named by the Greeks after the god of the city of Delphi. In Greek, consolida means "to strengthen" which adds meaning to a wedding where one hopes the matrimonial bond will strengthen the betrothed's commitment to each other.

Pink, white and blue varieties are the most dominant and most traditional, although red and mixed types can also be obtained. One of the pink varieties, the "Princess Caroline," so named because it was used at Princess Caroline of Monaco's wedding, is characterized by outstanding uniformity in both color and length. Like other pure and hybrid varieties, these delphinium have no scent.

EUCALYPTUS

The common name "eucalyptus" is the same as its botanical name. There are several varieties of eucalyptus available in either a green-gray or blue-green color. All are very aromatic. "Silver Dollar" is the type of eucalyptus traditionally used at weddings. Romantics believe that placing branches of this tree at a wedding will bring good fortune to the newlyweds.

Eucalyptus originated in Australia. It is available year-round and makes an interesting setting for many other varieties of flowers. Today eucalyptus is cultivated primarily in the United States and Israel. Eucalyptus oil was historically used in medication. It is considered good luck to have it at weddings as a symbol that the couple will enjoy good health together.

FREESIA

Freesia is one of the most popular flowers, possibly because it is so distinctive. The flower was named after a German doctor, F.F. Freese, who discovered it in Cape Colony in South Africa.

Freesia have long, narrow sword-shaped leaves that grow in two rows. The flower stalk is branched with 8-14 flowers growing from the top of the stalk at a 90 degree angle, forming a comb. Some compare this comb of flowers to a wedding party, with the two largest blooms signifying the bride and groom and the remaining buds the attendants.

A note of caution: handle freesia delicately. Like a bride, they must be treated gently and with respect if they are to flourish.

You can determine how fresh your freesia is by the number of flowers along the comb that are open. Remember, for a wedding it is best to have your flowers at their fullest bloom on your wedding day. This is one flower that appreciates some sugar in its water. Freesia can last for more than two weeks.

Freesia come in a wide palette of colors and are available throughout the year. White and yellow varieties predominate, although freesia are also available in shades of blue, red, purple, orange and pink. Freesia are often added to other, larger flowers in long cascading bouquets. Its blooms can also be separated and wired to headpieces or used in tight cluster designs.

GARDENIA

If ever there was a flower suited for a wedding party corsage, it is the gardenia. Its small and spotless white blooms appear to have been strategically placed against shiny leaves. This flower is dainty enough to complement any member of the bridal group's gown but impressive enough to make a statement. The fragrance of the gardenia flower is jasmine-like and projects a pleasant but not overpowering scent. Some bridal parties also use potted gardenia plants to set off the tables on which the reception seating arrangement cards are placed.

The gardenia was discovered in Asia by botanist A. Garden who brought them with him to England in the mid-1700s. Although these flowers are somewhat available in all parts of the world throughout the year, the great majority of the cut flowers are used in America. Since gardenias are primarily used in small personal carrying arrangements at weddings and then either pressed or dried as memories, their keeping time is unimportant.

GERBERA DAISY

The gerbera daisy is sometimes known as the African daisy or Transvaal daisy because of its origination in South Africa, where it was discovered by Dutch botanist Gronovius in 1737. He named the gerbera in honor of his Danish colleague Traugott Gerber. The flower is very similar in appearance to a field daisy but comes in a large variety of colors and sizes. The most popular colors are yellow, red, orange, pink, white and two-tone. There are more than 41 varieties available from Holland throughout the year.

With their bright and splashy appearance, gerbera are wonderful for informal weddings. Because of their broad range of sizes from standard to micro to mini, they are particularly attractive in table arrangements. One intriguing new standard variety is the "Fire Ball" which has a two-foot stem, is almost five inches in diameter and appears to be an amazing mass of orange flames. Since gerbera have a long vase life of 2-3 weeks, wedding party guests can enjoy them long after the wedding.

POPULAR WEDDING FLOWERS

GLADIOLUS

This flower adds majesty to any large arrangement at a wedding. Gladiolus are often used in tall fabric -covered vases to line the bridal aisle to the altar. Since they have no scent, they make excellent decorative flowers to enhance the look of food serving areas at the reception. Experienced floral designers can also take individual blooms from the gladiolus and create a camellia-like flower known as a "glamellia" for use as corsages and boutonnieres.

The species was discovered growing wild in Africa. It was brought back to Europe in bulb form by amateur horticulturists and was later improved and domesticated by professional breeders. Today, the gladiolus is known as a glad in some parts of the United States and as a sword lily in other areas.

The color palette of the flower and its gradations of shading are so varied that it can easily fit into any wedding color scheme. You can choose from red, white, yellow, pink, violet, orange, and purple varieties. The flowers grow in clusters up its sword-like stem, with the larger flowers appearing closer to the bottom. This makes it an excellent flower for table settings since the beauty of the flower can easily be enjoyed at eye level. Glads are available year-round but are most plentiful in the summer.

IRIS

The iris, in its undeveloped form, was discovered in Africa in the late-1800s. However, once it was brought to Holland and hybridized, it truly took a position in the world of flowers. That importance was recognized in the scientific name given to the flower, Iris Hollandica. The name iris itself translates into "rainbow," as strong multiple colors are among the flower's top notes of interest.

The iris has an unusual leaf-colored stem that runs up its entire two-foot stem. Atop this stem is a single blossom which features turned-back petals and a contrasting color comb. Dutch iris will keep for an entire week. The most popular iris is of a blazing dark blue color. However, there is growing interest in the yellow, white and two-tone varieties. Make note of the strength of color in buying iris. If the color is faint, it may indicate that the buds will have difficulty opening in time for the ceremony.

There are many legends surrounding the significance of iris at weddings. Perhaps the most interesting is that a blue iris and a white iris are placed in a bud vase at the bride's table to remind her that her marriage would have both vibrant and pale times. It is said that this started the traditional pledge that marriages are for better or for worse.

LIATRIS

The liatris grows to as much as 16 inches and features a lavender-pink flower. The flower spike is tube-like and opens from the top down. Depending on where in the United States you are from, the liatris is also called a gayfeather, a blazing star, or a button snakeroot. The flower was originally grown in the eastern section of America but was formally cultivated in England around 1734. The vertical erectness of the liatris and its long vase life of about two weeks make this flower popular for vase and floral arrangements at weddings. The liatris is odorless and best used in modern floral arrangements.

LILIES (ASIATIC AND ORIENTAL)

No flower is more frequently used at weddings than this hybrid. These lilies were originally found in China and Japan. The first known use of lilies at weddings was by the Ming Dynasty in China.

Asiatics come in a wider color selection than the Orientals. These include yellow, pink, peach, ivory and white as well as combinations of these colors. The Asiatic is smaller than the Oriental lily, although each contains 3-7 flowers per stem.

Two of the most popular lilies are the "Stargazer" and the "Casablanca." The Stargazer is noted for its red accent marks, which highlight the white throat of this orchid-like flower. The Casablanca is a huge white flower which takes its name from the Spanish "casa" (house) and "blanca" (white). They are found throughout the world.

Lilies are strongly scented. The Oriental hybrids are more heavily scented than the Asiatic varieties. One must be careful to keep them separate and apart from other fragrant flowers. They are versatile enough to be used in bouquets, floral arrangements, altar decorations and church aisle decorations.

There are over 4,000 lily varieties. Among the new popular varieties used in American weddings is the "La Rive," which has a very soft pink coloration. White lilies are often used as a single flower placed upon a white wedding Bible. Because they vary so greatly in color and are available to some extent throughout the year, there is a lily for every bride.

Warning: Put a protective shield under the lily when using them as corsages. The anthers that project from the center of the flower will easily stain fabric. It is safest to remove the anther prior to using them in this manner.

LILY OF THE VALLEY

Wedding bells traditionally proclaim a marriage. Perhaps this explains why the lily of the valley is found at most weddings. It is popularly used in bridal bouquets and other arrangements because its flowers are reminiscent of wedding bells. Like a bride and groom, its oval basal leaves stand in pairs around a pendulous stalk. The flower cluster of 4-10 white, bell-shaped blooms sits atop the stalk much as church bells are at the top of the steeple.

POPULAR WEDDING FLOWERS

Botanically known as Convallaria majalis, this delicate-looking perennial was first seen growing in Western Europe in May, 1420. This makes sense since May is the only month in which it blooms naturally. Today most of the supply is still from Western Europe. However, current technology permits bridal parties to obtain it year-round.

If lily of the valley is to be used in vases, it is best to put the whole flower, including the roots, in the water. This will allow you to enjoy it for about 5 days.

LISIANTHUS

Lisianthus is more commonly referred to as eustoma. Part of its appeal is its large size. In fact, its very name means wide open mouth. The four-petaled blossom presents itself in a saucer shape with a single stamen and seed capsule apparent in its center. The ornamental flower sits atop a 30- to 32-inch stem with opposing oval leaves. Some are single flowered varieties, others double.

The eustoma found its way to Europe and the United States from Japan. It is available in dark purple, pink, white, and two-tone. The flowers make a dramatic addition to arrangements. Since each flower is very large, just a few can add drama to entryway and table displays. While most varieties are available from May through December, some varieties, such as "Dark Blue Fuji," can be obtained year-round. Lisianthus can last 3-4 weeks.

NARCISSUS

See description for daffodil.

NERINE

The nerine, also known as the spider lily, is primarily available in pink, although it is also available in red, orange and white. It is a bulbous plant which originated in the coastal regions of South Africa. Its botanical name is after the Greek sea god, Nereus. Legend has it that the bulb was placed aboard ships to be traded and that some of them were hijacked to the Isle of Guernsey where they proliferate today.

The leaves of nerine are about 10 inches long. The average 16-inch flower stalk bears a cluster of 6-10 trumpet-shaped blooms with rather undulating flower lobes. Each flower is 1-3 inches in diameter.

As a complete flower, the nerine's height, erectness, and rather open, airy appearance make it a good choice for those wanting a more contemporary look to their wedding design. Individually, its flowers can be used for corsages for the wedding party. It is available year-round. The flowers last for more than one week.

One of the most popular varieties is "Pink Triumph." Perhaps the nerine is used to symbolize the triumph of the young girl winning her favorite guy.

ORCHID (CATTLEYA)

The variety of orchid most commonly seen in the United States is a hybrid called cattleya. Named after a British merchant, the cattleya is a relatively expensive and fragile flower. For this reason, it has traditionally been reserved for very special occasions, such as weddings, where it is commonly used as the focal point for the bridal bouquet or as a corsage for the mother of the bride and the mother of the groom.

Native to South America and grown worldwide today, this variety is available year-round in lavender, white, yellow, and orange. The flower itself makes a statement. Its lip, with beautiful markings, is usually a darker color than the other petals.

The flower grows on a stalk that is 4-6 inches in length, although most times the stem is cut and the flower is worn as a corsage. Since the flower itself is about eight inches in diameter, it can be worn alone and still look impressive. Although orchids can last about a week, they are easily damaged.

ORCHID (CYMBIDIUM)

There are many varieties of orchids. Some varieties, such as the cymbidium and dendrobian, are very versatile. Both are excellent for arrangements, corsages, and bouquets. Cymbidiums are particularly spectacular when used in a hand-tied bouquet or in a slight cascade for the bridal attendants. The regal dendrobian works well when incorporated into the ceremony design.

Cymbidium orchids are ancestors of the orchid hybrids. They come in both large and small flowered varieties. Large flowered varieties originated in Burma, India, and the Himalayas, while the small flowered varieties are native to Taiwan and China. The dendrobian orchid was originally discovered in Australia and eastern Indonesia.

Cymbidiums stand 12-32 inches high. Large flowered varieties carry 8-18 flowers on the stem, each measuring 4-6 inches in diameter, while two-thirds of the stem of the small flowered varieties is crowded with flowers. Dendrobian orchid stalks are at least a foot long. Each contains 8-12 flowers measuring 3 1/2 to almost 5 inches in diameter. This variety is butterfly-shaped on a long stem. The flower is generally lavender or white.

Available year-round, cymbidium and dendrobian orchids have no scent. In order to ensure a 2-5 week life for cymbidiums, they should be kept out of the sun. Dendrobians are particularly sensitive to pollution. They last 8-12 days.

POPULAR WEDDING FLOWERS

PEONY

Peonies give spring weddings a unique, elegant look and aroma. The cultivation of peonies began in China more than 1,000 years ago; however, its name is derived from the doctor of the Greek gods and alludes to its medicinal qualities.

There is only a six-week window, between May and June, during which peonies can be purchased, although this time frame is expanding somewhat. Its limited availability period adds to its uniqueness in wedding centerpiece arrangements. Its soft yet elegant composition imparts dignity and femininity to wedding designs. Peonies retain their beauty for up to two weeks.

Peonies are usually double-flowered with a diameter of about six inches. The 30 varieties generally available are most popularly found in white, red, and pink. By far the most popular peony is the pink "Sarah Bernhardt," which accounts for half of all peonies. Other popular varieties are the white "Shirley Temple," the bright pink "Dr. Arthur Fleming," and the red "Karl Rosenfield." The white "Duchesse de Nemours" variety has a strong fragrance. New early flowering varieties are being introduced in salmon-orange, orange-red, and cream-white. These, too, are named for famous people.

PINCUSHION

The pincushion flower is so named because its center appears to be a pincushion filled with pins. A perennial summer bloom, it contains three-inch round flowers on two-foot stems. At one time, the flower stems were weak, impacting their usability, but this problem has been overcome through breeding.

Its botanical name, Scabiosa, derives from the skin disease "scabies" for which it was thought to be a remedy. Originally cultivated in the Mediterranean regions, it requires a temperate climate or summer temperatures. Perhaps part of its decorative appeal is that it is available for only 3-4 months of the year.

Scabiosa is primarily purchased in shades of lavender blue, violet blue and white, although it originally was found naturally in a crimson color. The flower has a frilly petal that is very feminine. It is frequently used in table arrangements because of its pleasing shape and striking blue color. It has no scent. Its vase life is 3-7 days.

PROTEA

Brides and grooms are the king and queen of their night. Perhaps this is well symbolized by using protea in wedding arrangements. The king protea (cynaroides) and queen protea (magnifica) are large, with well-formed flower heads. As with people, the king is often taller than his queen; the king achieving 2-3 feet in length and the queen 1 1/2 - 2 feet. There are also smaller varieties.

A protea is a honey pot or sugar bush. It is a woody plant that was originally cultivated in Australia, Israel and southern parts of Africa. Its leaves are simple and alternate. The shape of the flower is irregular with four external segments which grow alternately with the petals. The flowers are somewhat arched inwards. The center is double and surrounded by hairy bracts. Some varieties are black topped. Some have a woolly appearance.

The long-lasting protea makes a dramatic statement when used in low table arrangements. They are most appropriately used in contemporary wedding design. Protea's eye-catching appeal will be wasted if your arrangement is elevated, as its beauty lies in its compact form and coloration, which is best appreciated at low levels.

QUEEN ANNE'S LACE

The name says it all. Delicate and lacy, Queen Anne's Lace looks like the lace used in bridal gown design. It is a white, flat flower comprised of hundreds of small florets on a straight 1 1/2- to 3- foot stem. Actually, it is a summer wildflower that grows in the field, and most florists do not carry it. But do not gather it directly from a field as it may bear chiggers or other small critters. Once picked, it has a life span of only about three days. Apart from informal wildflower arrangements, it can also be used in the hair to complement the wedding gown.

RANUNCULUS

A ranunculus is like a very full peony. This early spring flower originated in the Persian Gulf and is sometimes called a Persian buttercup or Iranian peony. The ranunculus name is from the latin rana, meaning "frog." It was so named because the flower grows best in swampy areas.

This flower is extremely full and tightly packed with petals. It is available in multiple shades of orange, red, pink, yellow, and white.

Ranunculus are up to four inches across and sit on 10- to 18- inch stems. The flower was frequently used by Persian shahs to decorate the bridal suite. These brightly colored, unscented flowers will last more than a week with proper care.

ROSES

No flower symbolizes love more than the rose, making it the perfect wedding flower. Fittingly, among the more than 130 popular varieties are the "Bridal Pink," "Darling," "Kiss," "Flirt," and "Only Love."

POPULAR WEDDING FLOWERS

Many varieties are named for women, although roses today are often given to men by women as a symbol of their love. Perhaps due to their names, "Purple Prince" and "Idole" are popular choices for men. Rose varieties can be categorized as large flowered, medium flowered, small flowered, or cluster. Some are heavily scented; some moderately; some lightly; and some have no scent at all. Depending upon the variety, roses can last up to three weeks.

The rose is from the family Rosaceae. It is naturally a prickly shrub with feathery leaves and showy flowers having five petals in the wild state but often being doubled or partly doubled under cultivation. The thorns on the stalks vary depending on the variety. The stalk length runs between 12 inches and 40 inches, depending upon variety and quality. The leaves are compound and may consist of five leaflets. They can be obtained in reds, pinks, salmon, orange, lavender, cream, white, and two-tone colors.

Some rose varieties were first seen in Asia; others in Central Europe, the Middle East, and Asia Minor. They can easily be used for any phase of wedding design: altar and church decorations, corsages and boutonnieres, hand bouquets, and centerpieces. Roses can be used to complement any wedding decor. For example, the "Porcelina" rose, which is a large, ivory-colored flower, can be used to create an elegant bridal bouquet, eliciting a formal atmosphere.

The softly colored "Champagne" rose singly wrapped in a napkin at each dinner plate is a nice touch to symbolize your affection and appreciation for your guests. Warning: make sure to remove all thorns!

SAPONARIA

The name of this flower is derived from the Latin word for soap because the sap of the plant is said to have a cleansing effect. It was originally used in weddings as a sign that the bride was cleansed or pure.

Although first found in the Mediterranean region, saponaria today is primarily field-grown in the Netherlands. It is a very delicate, small flower on long, flowing stems. It is used as a filler in bouquets because of the abundance of flowers on each stalk. Deep pink is the most commonly used variety, but it is also available in pure white. Both its colors and its delicate scent make this flower popular for use in weddings. It is only available in June, July and August, but the flower can be forced indoors for weddings in late May.

SNAPDRAGON

The botanical name for snapdragon is Antirrhinum majus. It originated in the Mediterranean region of France and Spain more than 400 years ago. It is now one of the most popular flowers around. The flowers sit in graduated clusters atop a spike that is between 8 and 12 inches in length and along a stem that can grow as long as 45 inches. Snapdragons are available in shades of red, orange, lavender, pink, salmon, and white. They have no scent.

Because of their abundance of color and their vertical shape, snapdragons are extremely useful in vase arrangements. These flowers are readily available in May and June and then again in late summer until the end of October. Snapdragons can also be found in limited supply in late winter and early spring. Properly cared for, they can last about a week.

Note of warning: these flowers require sufficient water supply at all times. They are also extremely sensitive to ethylene gas and should be kept far away from fruits and vegetables on food table displays. If kept too close, they will start to drop their buds on the table.

SPEEDWELL

The scientific name of Speedwell is Veronica longifolia. It's a very old plant and the first record of its cultivation was in Switzerland/France in the mid 1500s.

The flower itself is primarily blue and grows cone-shaped sitting above heart-shaped leaves. It must be carefully cared for. Otherwise, it has the tendency to dry out and become limp. There are some pink and white varieties grown in Virginia. These flowers have the same tendency to dry out and must be carefully pre-treated.

Speedwell is available only in the heat of the summer. The flower is primarily used in mixed bouquets and basic floral arrangements. The Veronica longifolia has a limited vase life of about five days.

STAR OF BETHLEHEM

The Star of Bethlehem, botanically known as Ornithogalum, features white flowers with either a white-green or a black-grey center. A series of two dozen or more flowers sit pyramid-shape atop a stem that is approximately 15 inches long. These flowers originated in Africa but were formally cultivated in Holland 450 years ago.

The star of Bethlehem was so named because it reminded the priests of flowers that were found in churches of the sacred city of Bethlehem. In medieval times, this flower was used to signify the religious commitment of the bride to the groom.

The star of Bethlehem was a rarely used flower until about 50 years ago, when florists discovered that its flowers could be easily adapted to dye in a variety of shades. These flowers are strong and will maintain their presence for up to a month. Although this flower is normally long-lived, it is particularly sensitive to fruits and vegetables. Therefore it is advisable not to use it on tables that feature edibles. These flowers look particularly nice in small bud vases and are frequently used to decorate cocktail tables.

POPULAR WEDDING FLOWERS

STATICE

Statice or limonium gives the appearance of a sea of color. Perhaps that is why it is also known as sea lavender. Statice used to be predominantly yellow, but today most varieties are seen in shades of blue. They are also available in purple, lavender, white, and pink.

Statice originated in Turkestan and areas in the Mediterranean. Botanically, blue sea lavender is called Statice perezii. It was named after the Dutch baron P.J.R. de Perez, who was Governor of the Dutch West Indies from 1803 to 1859. This variety is distinguished by its smooth, bare stalk, comprised of multi-branching stems of small, star-shaped flower clusters.

The other major variety consists primarily of purple flowers with a splash of white. Both are used as filler flowers in large arrangements and are the perfect addition to any natural-looking wedding design. Statice lasts about two weeks and dries well, so the bride can have a beautiful keepsake of her wedding. It is available year-round.

STEPHANOTIS

Pure white and fragrant, this traditional wedding flower has been used in bridal bouquets, corsages, and wedding decorations for centuries. Sometimes referred to as Madagascar jasmine, it is delicately fragranced and has a pure white waxy color. Although it is relatively expensive and must be handled carefully to avoid bruising, stephanotis is perfect for wedding use any time of the year.

Originally from Madagascar and first introduced in England at the beginning of the 19th century, stephanotis is actually an evergreen climbing shrub with long tendrils and shiny dark green leaves that average 2 1/2 inches. Each star-shaped flower cluster is formed from five tips of petals sitting atop a tube which protrudes from a short stem. Each individual flower itself is less than two inches.

STOCK

Stock traces its origins to ancient times. This extremely fragrant, spiked flower has a hairy clustered appearance. The flowers are available in white, red, pink, salmon, lavender, and yellow. It is extremely useful in mixed bridal bouquets and large arrangements because its blooms are so tightly packed. A skilled floral designer can also transform this inexpensive flower into a wisteria-looking vine to drape an arch or trellis.

Stock, also called gillyflowers, are botanically identified as Matthiola. They are available throughout most of the year, with lesser amounts of the assortment during the Thanksgiving and Christmas seasons. Matthiola will last at least one week.

SUNFLOWER

Americans have fallen in love with sunflowers. Botanically, a sunflower is called Helianthus, coming from the Greek words "helio," meaning sun, and "anthos," meaning flowers.

The flower is self descriptive. From its dark-colored center, yellow ray-like petals project out much like the sun's rays. Helianthus is one of the few major flowers that found its origin in the United States. These flowers grow wild in the southwest and are now professionally cultivated throughout the world.

Giant varieties can have flower heads that are 15 inches in diameter. Because of their huge size, giant helianthus are best suited to single placement or in large arrangements. Smaller varieties measuring 3-4 inches across make excellent filler and can be worn in the hair during informal ceremonies. These fragrance-free flowers will last up to 12 days.

SWEET PEA

This vividly colored, climbing flower is a native of Italy. Its scientific name is Lathyrus. Since its colors are strong oranges, lilacs and purples and its flowers are extremely fragrant, Italian royalty used this as part of the altar setting at weddings. One common variety identifies this wedding connection through the name "Royal Family."

Once the flowers were cultivated professionally, breeders eliminated much of their scent. Now smaller sweet peas have absolutely no fragrance. Most varieties of sweet peas are readily available in the spring.

TUBEROSE

Often confused with snapdragon, tuberose is a small, rose-like bud flower which grows atop three-foot stems. This flower has many fragrant florets which grow and open from the bottom up and look a bit like stephanotis. The maximum size of each white, star-shaped flower is 2 1/2 inches when fully opened.

Tuberose originated in southern Mexico and is now grown primarily in Israel, Africa, and the south of France. An extremely fragrant flower, it is frequently used for corsages and small bouquets. It can also be used to decorate small cocktail tables at the wedding reception.

In fact, tuberose flowers are so fragrant that they are in great demand by the perfume industry in France. Due to their limited availability and perfume industry demands, they can be quite expensive.

POPULAR WEDDING FLOWERS

TULIPS

For variety of shape and color, few flowers surpass the tulip. Hundreds of species of tulips originally grew wild in Turkey and Iran. They were first formally cultivated in the Netherlands in the 1500s. At one time, this flower was so highly valued that it was used as money. At that period of time, extremely wealthy Holland traders used tulips at weddings as a sign of affluence.

Botanically called "Tulipa," its name is derived from the turban shape of the flower. Today there are thousands of different species available at different times of the year. They are cupped, fringed, spiked, single-colored, multicolored, large and small. All are stately adornments in large and small floral arrangements.

A popular and yet unusual tulip is the "Parakeet" tulip, which has irregularly shaped, two-tone streaked petals on flowers that are so large that they have to be braced so as not to collapse their stems. Another is the "Kees Nelis Triumph" tulip, which features a dramatic red cup petal that appears to change instantly into a flaming yellow border. Since tulips are available in greatest abundance in the spring, they are sought after as wedding decor to symbolize a new beginning.

Since limited life span does not adversely affect wedding use, the tulip is a wedding standard. However, their hollow stems restrict them to floral designs with a water source. A special note of care: avoid mixing tulips with daffodils in the same arrangement. These flowers are allergic to each other.

WAXFLOWER

The waxflower, or Chamelaucium ciliatum, is sometimes known as the pink tea tree. It is a very small, light, airy flower with a diameter that is less than an inch. Each branching stem contains many buds. Its foliage is needlelike.

Because of the delicate nature of its flowers, the waxflower is frequently used as filler in floral design. Its primary use is in bouquets and as decoration for a bridal table. It is available in pink, lavender, and white. It is available starting in December and may be easily obtained through the end of May.

Historically, the waxflower was used as a setting for tea service when the bride-to-be was formally introduced to the groom's parents.

Allium sphaerocephalon
drumstick Allium

Alstroemeria hybrid
Peruvian lily

Alstroemeria hybrid
Peruvian lily

Alstroemeria hybrid
Peruvian lily

Amaryllis belladonna
belladonna lily

Anemone coronaria
'Mona Lisa' group
Anemone

Aster hybrid
Butterfly series

Callistephus chinensis
'Matsumoto'
Matsumoto **Aster**

Gypsophila paniculata
'Gilboa'
baby's breath

POPULAR WEDDING FLOWERS

Gypsophila paniculata
miniature **baby's breath**

Centaurea cyanus
bachelor's button

Craspedia globosa
billy buttons

Strelitzia reginae
bird of paradise

Bouvardia hybrid
'Lady Stephanie'

Bouvardia ternifolia
Bouvardia

Zantedeschia elliottiana
yellow mini-**calla**

Zantedeschia rehmannii
burgundy mini-**calla**

Zantedeschia aethiopica
'Alba'
calla

Dianthus caryophyllus
hybrid 'Tapestry'
carnation

Dianthus caryophyllus
nana 'Porcelain'
miniature **carnation**

Chrysanthemum
frutescens
marguerite daisy

Chrysanthemum
morifolium
'Westland Yellow'

Chrysanthemum
morifolium 'Red Rover'
red rover mum

Chrysanthemum
morifolium
'Statesman'

Celosia argentea
v. cristata
crested cockscomb

Narcissus hybrid
daffodil

Dahlia hybrid
formal decorative Dahlia

POPULAR WEDDING FLOWERS

Delphinium ajacis
pink larkspur

Delphinium
'belladonna' group

Delphinium hybrid
'Pacific Giant'
hybrid Delphinium

Eucalyptus polyanthemos
'Flat Seed'
silver dollar Eucalyptus

Freesia hybrid
pink

Freesia hybrid
red/rust

Freesia hybrid
white

Freesia hybrid
yellow

Gardenia jasminoides
Gardenia

Gerbera jamesonii
Germini 'Foxi'
mini Gerbera

Gerbera jamesonii
'Tamara'
Gerbera

Gerbera jamesonii
'Sensitive'
Gerbera

Gladiolus hybrid
gladiola

Gladiolus hybrid
gladiola

Gladiolus x. colvillei
mini glads

Iris hybrid
'Casa Blanca'
Iris

Iris hybrid
'Professor Blaauw'
Iris

Liatris callilepis
gayfeather

POPULAR WEDDING FLOWERS

Lilium Asiatic hybrid
'Mercedes'
Asiatic **lily**

Lilium Asiatic hybrid
'Polyanne'
Asiatic **lily**

Lilium speciosum hybrid
'Casa Blanca'
Oriental **Lily**

Lilium speciosum hybrid
'Stargazer'
Oriental **lily**

Convallaria majalis
lily-of-the-valley

Eustoma grandiflorum
Echo series
double white **lisianthus**

Eustoma grandiflorum
pink **lisianthus**

Narcissus hybrid
'Paperwhite'
Paperwhites

Nerine bowdenii
Nerine

Cattleya x. hybrid
'Semi-Alba'
Cattleya **orchid**

Cattleya x. Japhette
Japhette **orchid**

Cymbidium
hybrid mini
mini-Cymbidium **orchid**

Cymbidium hybrid
Cymbidium **orchid**

Cymbidium hybrid
Cymbidium **orchid**

Phalaenopsis amabilis
Phalaenopsis **orchid**

Paeonia officinalis
hybrid
peony

Scabiosa caucasica
perennial **pincushion** flower

Protea cynaroides
King Protea

POPULAR WEDDING FLOWERS

Protea magnifica
'Rose Queen'
Queen Protea

Ammi majus
Queen Anne's lace

Ranunculus asiaticus
Persian Ranunculus

Ranunculus asiaticus
Persian Ranunculus

Rosa hybrid
'Afterglow'
tea **rose**

Rosa hybrid
'Dolores'
tea **rose**

Rosa hybrid
'Kardinal'
tea **rose**

Rosa hybrid
'Lady Diane'
tea **rose**

Saponaria vaccaria
Saponaria

Antirrhinum majus
white **snapdragon**

Veronica longifolia
speedwell

Ornithogalum
umbellatum
star of Bethlehem

Limonium hybrid
'Misty' series
Misty white **statice**

Limonium sinuatum
blue **statice**

Stephanotis floribunda
Madagascar jasmine

Matthiola incana
lavender **stock**

Matthiola incana
peach **stock**

Matthiola incana
yellow **stock**

Helianthus annuus
'Sunbright'
sunflower

Helianthus annuus
sunflower

Lathyrus odoratus
sweet pea

Polianthes tuberosa
tuberose

Tulipa hybrid
purple **tulip**

Tulipa hybrid
'Flaming Parrot'
French parrot **tulip**

Tulipa hybrid
red **tulip**

Tulipa hybrid
white **tulip**

Chamelaucium uncinatum
'Purple Pride'
waxflower

"To love someone deeply gives you strength."
~ Lao Tzu

TABLE CENTERPIECES..193
BALLOONS 194

DECORATIONS

PHOTO: KAREN FRENCH

DECORATIONS

DECORATIONS CAN ENHANCE YOUR WEDDING by unifying all of the components of your ceremony and reception. Decorations can range anywhere from floral arrangements, twinkling lights, and centerpieces to more personal touches such as seating cards, menus, favors, and more. Most items, from stationery to place settings, are purchased or arranged based on a unified theme. For example, if the theme is Asian inspired, paper lanterns and take-out boxes can create beautiful "Japanese style" ambience.

TABLE CENTERPIECES

Each of the tables at your reception, including the head table, should be decorated with a centerpiece.

Options: Candles, mirrors, and flowers are popular choices for table centerpieces. However, the options are endless. Just be creative! An arrangement of shells, for example, makes a very nice centerpiece for a seaside reception. Votive candles set on top of a mirror make a romantic centerpiece for an evening reception.

A wreath of greenery woven with colored ribbon makes a delightful centerpiece. Use a different color ribbon at each table and have your guests seated according to ribbon color!

Things to Consider: Select a table centerpiece which complements your colors and/or setting. The centerpiece for the head table should be larger or more elaborate than the ones for the other tables. Make sure that your centerpiece is kept low enough so as not to hinder conversation among guests seated across from each other. Consider using a centerpiece that your guests can take home as a memento of your wedding.

Tips to Save Money: Make your own table centerpieces using materials that are not expensive.

Price Range: $10 - $100 each

DECORATIONS

BALLOONS

Balloons are often used to decorate a reception site. A popular idea is to release balloons at the church or reception. This adds a festive, exciting, and memorable touch to your wedding. Balloons can be used to create an arch backdrop for the wedding cake or inexpensive centerpieces for the tables.

Things to Consider: Color coordinate your balloons to match your color scheme. Choose colors from your bouquet or your bridesmaids' dresses. Balloons should be delivered and set up well in advance—at least before the photographer shows up.

If you are planning to release balloons at the church or reception, check with your city. Releasing balloons in some cities might be illegal. Also make sure there are no wires where balloons can get entangled. If they do, you could be held responsible for damages or clean-up expenses.

Tips to Save Money: Balloons are less expensive than fresh flowers and can be used as a substitute for flowers to decorate the reception site.

Price Range: $75 - $500

"Where you find true friendship,
you find true love."
~ Anonymous

TRANSPORTATION...195

TRANSPORTATION COMPARISON CHART 196

WEDDING DAY TRANSPORTATION CHART...................198

TRANSPORTATION

PHOTO: LARRY MONET

PHOTO: RYAN PHILLIPS PHOTOGRAPHY

PHOTO: KAREN FRENCH

PHOTO: ANDY MARCUS

PHOTO: KAREN FRENCH

TRANSPORTATION

IT IS CUSTOMARY FOR THE BRIDE AND HER FATHER TO RIDE TO THE CEREMONY site together on the wedding day. You may also include some or all members of your wedding party. Normally a procession to the church begins with the bride's mother and several of the bride's attendants in the first vehicle. If desired, you can provide a second vehicle for the rest of the attendants. The bride and her father will go in the last vehicle. This vehicle will also be used to transport the bride and groom to the reception site after the ceremony.

TRANSPORTATION

Options: There are various options for transportation. The most popular choice is a limousine since it is big and open and can accommodate several people, as well as your bridal gown. You can also choose to rent a car that symbolizes your personality as a couple.

There are luxury cars such as Mercedes Benz, sports cars such as a Ferraris, and vintage vehicles such as 1950s Thunderbirds or 1930s Cadillacs. If your ceremony and reception sites are fairly close together, and if weather permits, you might want to consider a more romantic form of transportation, such as a horse-drawn carriage.

Things to Consider: In some areas of the country, limousines are booked on a three-hour minimum basis.

Beware: Make sure the company you choose is fully licensed and has liability insurance. Do not pay the full amount until after the event.

Tips to Save Money: Consider hiring only one large limousine. This limousine can transport you, your parents, and your attendants to the ceremony, and then you and your new husband from the ceremony to the reception.

Price Range: $35 - $100 per hour

TRANSPORTATION COMPARISON CHART

QUESTIONS	POSSIBILITY 1	POSSIBILITY 2
What is the name of the transportation service?		
What is the website and e-mail of the transportation service?		
What is the address of the transportation service?		
What is the name and phone number of my contact person?		
How many years have you been in business?		
How many vehicles do you have available?		
Can you provide a back-up vehicle in case of an emergency?		
What types of vehicles are available?		
What are the various sizes of vehicles available?		
How old are the vehicles?		
How many drivers are available?		
Can you show me photos of your drivers?		
How do your drivers dress for weddings?		
Do you have liability insurance?		
What is the minimum amount of time required to rent a vehicle?		
What is the cost per hour? Two hours? Three hours?		
How much gratuity is expected?		
What is your payment/cancellation policy?		

TRANSPORTATION COMPARISON CHART

POSSIBILITY 3	POSSIBILITY 4	POSSIBILITY 5	POSSIBILITY 6

WEDDING DAY TRANSPORTATION CHART

TO CEREMONY SITE

NAME	Pickup Time	Pickup Location	Vehicle/Driver
Bride			
Groom			
Bride's Parents			
Groom's Parents			
Bridesmaids			
Ushers			
Other:			
Other:			
Other:			

TO RECEPTION SITE

NAME	Pickup Time	Pickup Location	Vehicle/Driver
Bride and Groom			
Bride's Parents			
Groom's Parents			
Bridesmaids			
Ushers			
Other:			
Other:			

"Love and you shall be loved."
~ Ralph Waldo Emerson

RENTAL ITEMS..199

GIFTS 209

PARTIES 211

MISCELLANEOUS 213

TIMELINES 225

WEDDING TRADITIONS...235

DO'S & DON'TS...239

WEDDING PARTY RESPONSIBILITIES 243

WHO PAYS FOR WHAT..249

WEDDING FORMATIONS 251

THINGS TO BRING..257

WEDDING PLANNING CALENDAR 259

RENTAL ITEMS, GIFTS & MORE

RENTAL ITEMS

NOT ALL ITEMS NEED TO BE PURCHASED FOR THE ceremony and reception. There are many items that you have the option of renting, such as a tent, canopy, chairs, and linens for the reception. This allows you to host a reception in your own home or in less traditional locations, such as an art museum, a local park, or at the beach. Be sure to take into account the cost for all these rental items when creating your budget.

BRIDAL SLIP

The bridal slip is an undergarment which gives the bridal gown its proper shape.

Things to Consider: Be sure to wear the same slip you'll be wearing on your wedding day during your fittings. Many bridal salons rent slips. Schedule an appointment to pick up your slip one week before the wedding; otherwise, you run the risk of not having one available on your wedding day. If rented, the slip will have to be returned shortly after the wedding. Arrange for someone to do this for you within the allotted time.

Tips to Save Money: Rent a slip rather than purchasing one; chances are you will never use it again.

Price Range: $25 - $75

CEREMONY ACCESSORIES

Ceremony rental accessories are the additional items needed for the ceremony but not included in the ceremony site fee.

Options: Ceremony rental accessories may include the following items:

Aisle Runner: A thin rug made of plastic, paper or cloth extending the length of the aisle. It is rolled out after the mothers are seated, just prior to the processional. Plastic or paper doesn't work well on grass; but if you must use one of these types of runners, make sure the grass is clipped short.

Kneeling Cushion: A small cushion or pillow placed in front of the altar where the bride and groom kneel for their wedding blessing.

RENTAL ITEMS

Arch (Christian): A white lattice or brass arch where the bride and groom exchange their vows, often decorated with flowers and greenery.

Chuppah (Jewish): A canopy under which a Jewish ceremony is performed, symbolizing cohabitation and consummation.

You may also need to consider renting audio equipment, aisle stanchions, candelabra, candles, candle-lighters, chairs, heaters, a gift table, a guest book stand, and a canopy.

Things to Consider: If you plan to rent any accessories for your ceremony, make sure the rental supplier has been in business for a reasonable period of time and has a good reputation. Reserve the items you need well in advance. Find out the company's payment, reservation, and cancellation policies.

Some companies allow you to reserve emergency items, such as heaters or canopies, without having to pay for them unless needed, in which case you would need to call the rental company a day or two in advance to request the items. If someone else requests the items you have reserved, the company should give you the right of first refusal.

Tips to Save Money: When considering a ceremony outside of a church, figure the cost of rental items. Negotiate a package deal, if possible, by renting items for both the ceremony and the reception from the same supplier. Consider renting these items from your florist so you only have to pay one delivery fee.

Price Range: $100 - $500

TENT/CANOPY

A large tent or canopy may be required for receptions held outdoors to protect you and your guests from the sun or rain. Usually rented through party rental suppliers, tents and canopies can be expensive due to the labor involved in delivery and setup.

Options: Tents and canopies come in different sizes and colors. Depending on the shape of your reception area, you may need to rent several smaller canopies rather than one large one. Contact several party rental suppliers to discuss the options.

Things to Consider: Consider this cost when making a decision between an outdoor and an indoor reception. In cooler weather, heaters may also be necessary.

Tips to Save Money: Shop early and compare prices with several party rental suppliers.

Price Range: $300 - $5,000

DANCE FLOOR

A dance floor will be provided by most hotels and clubs. However, if your reception site does not have a dance floor, you may need to rent one through your caterer or a party rental supplier.

Things to Consider: When comparing prices of dance floors, include the delivery and setup fees.

Price Range: $100 - $600

TABLES/CHAIRS

You will have to provide tables and chairs for your guests if your reception site or caterer doesn't provide them as part of their package. For a full meal, you will have to provide tables and seating for all guests. For a cocktail reception, you only need to provide tables and chairs for approximately 30 to 50 percent of your guests. Ask your caterer or reception site manager for advice.

Options: There are various types of tables and chairs to choose from. The most commonly used chairs for wedding receptions are typically white wooden or plastic chairs. The most common tables for receptions are round tables that seat eight guests. The most common head table arrangement is several rectangular tables placed end-to-end to seat your entire wedding party on one side, facing your guests. Contact various party rental suppliers to find out what types of chairs and tables they carry, as well as their price ranges.

Things to Consider: When comparing prices of renting tables and chairs, include the cost of delivery and setup.

Tips to Save Money: Attempt to negotiate free delivery and setup with party rental suppliers in exchange for giving them your business.

Price Range: $3 - $10 per person

LINEN/TABLEWARE

You will also need to provide linens and tableware for your reception if your reception site or caterer does not provide them as part of their package.

Options: For a sit-down reception where the meal is served by waiters and waitresses, tables are usually set with a cloth (usually white, but may be color coordinated with the wedding), a centerpiece, and complete place settings. At a less formal buffet reception where guests serve themselves, tables are covered with a cloth, but place settings are not mandatory. The necessary plates and silverware may be located at the buffet table, next to the food.

RENTAL ITEMS

Things to Consider: Linens and tableware depend on the formality of your reception. When comparing prices of linens and tableware, include the cost of delivery and setup.

Price Range: $3 - $25 per person

HEATERS

You may need to rent heaters if your ceremony or reception will be held outdoors and if the temperature could drop below sixty-five degrees.

Options: There are electric and gas heaters, both of which come in different sizes. Gas heaters are more popular since they do not have unsightly and unsafe electric cords.

Price Range: $25 - $75

LANTERNS

Lanterns are often used at evening receptions.

Options: Many choices are available, from fire lanterns to electric ones.

Things to Consider: Consider the formality of the reception and choose the proper lighting to complement your decorations.

Price Range: $6 - $60/lamp

OTHER RENTAL ITEMS (TRASH CANS, GIFT TABLE, ETC.)

If your reception site or caterer doesn't provide them, you will need to purchase, rent, or borrow other miscellaneous items for your reception, such as trash cans, a gift table, trash bags, and so on.

NOTES

RENTAL SUPPLIER COMPARISON CHART

QUESTIONS	POSSIBILITY 1	POSSIBILITY 2
What is the name of the party rental supplier?		
What is the address of the party rental supplier?		
What is the web site and e-mail of the party rental supplier?		
What is the name and phone number of my contact person?		
How many years have you been in business?		
What are your hours of operation?		
Do you have liability insurance?		
What is the cost per item needed?		
What is the cost of pickup and delivery?		
What is the cost of setting up the items rented?		
When would the items be delivered?		
When would the items be picked up after the event?		
What is your payment policy?		
What is your cancellation policy?		

RENTAL SUPPLIER COMPARISON CHART

POSSIBILITY 3	POSSIBILITY 4	POSSIBILITY 5	POSSIBILITY 6

CEREMONY EQUIPMENT CHECKLIST

RENTAL SUPPLIER: Contact Person:

Website:

E-mail:

Address:

City: State: Zip Code:

Phone Number: Hours:

Payment Policy:

Cancellation Policy:

Delivery Time: Tear-Down Time:

Setup Time: Pickup Time:

QTY.	ITEM	Description	Price	Total
	Arch/Altar		$	$
	Canopy (Chuppah)		$	$
	Backdrops		$	$
	Floor Candelabra		$	$
	Candles		$	$
	Candle lighters		$	$
	Kneeling Bench		$	$
	Aisle Stanchions		$	$
	Aisle Runners		$	$
	Guest Book Stand		$	$
	Gift Table		$	$
	Chairs		$	$
	Audio Equipment		$	$
	Lighting		$	$
	Heating/Cooling		$	$
	Umbrellas/Tents		$	$
	Bug Eliminator		$	$
	Coat/Hat Rack		$	$
	Garbage Cans		$	$

RENTAL SUPPLIER: _____ Contact Person: _____

Web site: _____

E-mail: _____

Address: _____

City: _____ State: _____ Zip Code: _____

Phone Number: _____ Hours: _____

Payment Policy: _____

Cancellation Policy: _____

Delivery Time: _____ Tear-Down Time: _____

Setup Time: _____ Pickup Time: _____

QTY.	ITEM	Description	Price	Total
	Audio Equipment		$	$
	Cake Table		$	$
	Candelabras/Candles		$	$
	Canopies		$	$
	Coat/Hat Rack		$	$
	Dance Floor		$	$
	Bug Eliminator		$	$
	Garbage Cans		$	$
	Gift Table		$	$
	Guest Tables		$	$
	Heating/Cooling		$	$
	High/Booster Chairs		$	$
	Lighting		$	$
	Mirror Disco Ball		$	$
	Place Card Table		$	$
	Tents		$	$
	Umbrellas		$	$
	Visual Equipment		$	$
	Wheelchair Ramp		$	$

NOTES

GIFTS

GIFTS ARE A WONDERFUL WAY TO SHOW YOUR APPRECIATION to family, friends, members of your wedding party and to all those who have assisted you in your wedding planning process. Brides and grooms usually like to exchange something small yet meaningful. Keepsake items make wonderful gifts for members of the wedding party.

BRIDE'S GIFT

The bride's gift is traditionally given by the groom to the bride. It is typically a personal gift, such as a piece of jewelry.

Options: A string of pearls, a watch, pearl earrings, or a gold chain with a heart-shaped charm holding photos of the two of you.

Things to Consider: This gift is not necessary and should be given only if your budget allows.

Tips to Save Money: Consider omitting this gift. A pretty card from the groom proclaiming his eternal love for the bride is a very special, yet inexpensive gift.

Price Range: $50 - $500

GROOM'S GIFT

The groom's gift is traditionally given by the bride to the groom.

Options: A nice watch, an elegant pen set, or a dramatic photo of the bride framed in silver or crystal.

Things to Consider: This gift is not necessary and should be given only if your budget allows.

Tips to Save Money: Consider omitting this gift. A pretty card from the bride proclaiming her eternal love for the groom is a very special, yet inexpensive gift.

Price Range: $50 - $500

GIFTS

BRIDESMAIDS' GIFTS

Bridesmaids' gifts are given by the bride to her bridesmaids and maid of honor as a permanent keepsake of the wedding. The best gifts are those that can be used both during and after the wedding, such as jewelry.

Options: For bridesmaids' gifts, consider items of jewelry that can be worn during the wedding to give your wedding party a coordinated and elegant look. Choose the collection that most fits your style, then select the type and color of stone to match the color of your flowers and/or bridesmaids' dresses. We believe this is the perfect bridesmaids' gift!

Things to Consider: Bridesmaids' gifts are usually presented at the bridesmaids' luncheon, if there is one, or at the rehearsal dinner. The gift to the maid of honor may be similar to the bridesmaids' gifts, but should be a bit more expensive.

Tips to Save Money: Ask your photographer to take, at no extra charge, professional portraits of each bridesmaid and her escort for use as bridesmaids' gifts. Select a beautiful background that will remind your bridesmaids of the occasion, such as your cake table. Put the photo in a pretty frame. This makes a very special yet inexpensive gift for your attendants.

Price Range: $25 - $200 per gift

USHERS' GIFTS

Ushers' gifts are given by the groom to his ushers as a permanent keepsake of the wedding.

Options: For ushers' gifts, consider fancy pen sets, wallets, leather belts, silver frames, watches, and desk clocks.

Things to Consider: The groom should deliver his gifts to the ushers at the bachelor party or at the rehearsal dinner. The gift to the best man may be similar to the ushers' gifts, but should be a bit more expensive.

Tips to Save Money: Negotiate with your photographer to take, at no extra charge, professional portraits of each usher and his escort for use as ushers' gifts. Select a beautiful background that will remind your ushers of the occasion, such as your cake table.

Price Range: $25 - $200 per gift

PARTIES

WEDDINGS ARE OFTEN MUCH MORE THAN A DAYLONG CELEBRATION. There can be plenty of festivities before and even after the actual wedding day. Typically, the events that take place before a wedding include the engagement party, bridal shower, bachelor party, bridesmaids' luncheon, and rehearsal dinner. Some couples also like to have a brunch the day after the wedding to relax and relive the previous evening's celebration.

ENGAGEMENT PARTY

The engagement party is generally thrown by the bride's family to celebrate the big news. Gifts are not required at this party.

Things to Consider: If your schedule won't allow for it, an engagement party is by no means a requirement.

Options: An engagement party is typically held in your parents' home; however, renting a space or having dinner in a nice restaurant are also acceptable.

BRIDAL SHOWER

Traditionally, your wedding shower is thrown by your maid of honor and bridesmaids, unless they are a member of your immediate family. Because a shower is a gift-giving occasion, it is not considered socially acceptable for anyone in your immediate family to host this event. If your mother or sisters wish to be involved, have them offer to help with the cost of the event or offer their home for it. The agenda usually includes some games and gift-opening. Be sure to have someone keep track of which gift is from whom.

Things to Consider: You may have several showers thrown for you. When creating your guest lists, be sure not to invite the same people to multiple showers (the exception being members of the wedding party, who may be invited to all showers without the obligation of bringing a gift.) Only include people who have been invited to the wedding—the only exception to this is a work shower, to which all coworkers may be invited, whether or not they are attending the wedding.

Options: Tea parties, spa days, cocktail parties, and traditional at-home events are all options—these days even men are being invited as coed showers become more and more popular! Generally, an event is themed (lingerie, cooking, home decor), and the invitation should give guests an idea of what type of gift to bring.

BACHELOR PARTY

The bachelor party is a male-only affair typically organized by the best man. He is responsible for selecting the date and reserving the place and entertainment as well as inviting his male friends and family. Your best man should also assign responsibilities to the ushers, as they should help with the organization of this party.

Things to Consider: You often hear wild stories about bachelor parties being nights full of women and alcohol, however, these stories are actually quite rare. Most of the time, they are all lies or a big exaggeration of what really happened. It is not uncommon for the guys invited to the bachelor party to create these wild stories and make a vow of never telling the truth about how boring the party really was! However, make this party a memorable one. Make sure you do something different and enjoy it!

Options: Traditionally, a typical bachelor party would start with the young bachelor and his friends getting together for dinner and a fair amount of alcohol, followed by an evening of bar-hopping. As the bachelor age group becomes older (average bachelor age today is 27), this tradition has changed a bit. Now a bachelor party can be as simple as a group of guys getting together for dinner and drinks, a day of golfing, a casino day trip, or a cruise.

Beware: Your best man should not plan your bachelor party for the night before the wedding, since chances are that you will consume a fair amount of alcohol and stay up late. You don't want to have a hangover or be exhausted during your wedding. It is much more appropriate to have the bachelor party two or three nights before the wedding. Tell your best man that you will be busy the night before the wedding, just in case he is planning to surprise you. Your best man should designate a driver for you and for those who will be drinking alcohol. Remember, you and your best man are responsible for the well-being of everybody invited to the party.

BRIDESMAIDS' LUNCHEON

The bridesmaids' luncheon is given by the bride for her bridesmaids. It is not a shower; rather, it is simply a time for good friends to get together formally before the bride changes her status from single to married.

Things to Consider: You can give your bridesmaids their gifts at this gathering. Otherwise, plan to give them their gifts at the rehearsal dinner.

Price Range: $12 - $60 per person

REHEARSAL DINNER

It is customary that the groom's parents host a dinner party following the rehearsal, the evening before the wedding. The dinner usually includes the bridal party, their spouses or guests, both sets of parents, close family members, the officiant, and the wedding consultant and/or coordinator.

Options: The rehearsal dinner party can be held just about anywhere, from a restaurant, hotel, or private hall to the groom's parents' home.

Tips to Save Money: Restaurants specializing in Mexican food or pizza are fun yet inexpensive options.

Price Range: $10 - $100 per person

MISCELLANEOUS

WITH ALL THAT IS INVOLVED IN PLANNING A WEDDING, it is easy to forget some simple but necessary tasks. Be sure that you don't forget to consider or complete some of the following items.

NEWSPAPER ANNOUNCEMENTS

There are two types of announcements you can send to your local newspaper: one to announce your engagement and one to announce your wedding.

For your engagement announcement, send information to the newspapers, along with a photograph, right after your engagement or at least six weeks before the wedding. The photograph is usually the head and shoulders of the engaged couple. The photograph should be wallet-sized or larger, black and white, and glossy. Call your local newspapers to ask about their requirements. Some papers will not take orders over the phone, so you might have to mail the information or deliver it personally.

For your wedding announcement, send information to the newspapers, along with a photograph of either the bride alone or the bridal couple, at least three weeks before the wedding. Again, the photograph should be wallet-sized or larger, black and white, and glossy. Your photograph should show the way you will look the day of your wedding. The announcement should appear the day following the ceremony.

Things to Consider: If you and your fiancé grew up in different towns, consider sending announcements to the local papers of both towns. If either of you is having second thoughts about the wedding, cancel both announcements as soon as possible.

Tips to Save Money: If you don't mind having your wedding announced a few weeks after the wedding, you can send a photo from your actual wedding day. This will save you the cost and hassle of dressing up to have your photo taken before the wedding.

Price Range: $40 - $100 (depending on size)

MISCELLANEOUS

MARRIAGE LICENSE

Marriage license requirements are state-regulated and may be obtained from the County Clerk in most county courthouses.

Options: Some states (California and Nevada, for example) offer two types of marriage licenses: a public license and a confidential one. The public license is the most common one and requires a health certificate and a blood test. It can only be obtained at the County Clerk's office.

The confidential license is usually less expensive and does not require a health certificate or blood test. If offered, it can usually be obtained from most Justices of the Peace. An oath must be taken in order to receive either license.

Things to Consider: Requirements vary from state to state, but generally include the following points:

1. Applying for and paying the fee for the marriage license. There is usually a waiting period before the license is valid and a limited time before it expires.

2. Meeting residency requirements for the state and/or county where the ceremony will take place.

3. Meeting the legal age requirements for both bride and groom or having parental consent.

4. Presenting any required identification, birth or baptismal certificates, marriage eligibility, or other documents.

5. Obtaining a medical examination and/or blood test for both the bride and groom to detect communicable diseases.

Price Range: $20 - $100

PRENUPTIAL AGREEMENT

A prenuptial agreement is a legal contract between the bride and groom itemizing the property each brings into the marriage and explaining how those properties will be divided in case of divorce or death. Although you can write your own agreement, it is advisable to have an attorney draw up or review the document. The two of you should be represented by different attorneys.

Things to Consider: Consider a prenuptial agreement if one or both of you have a significant amount of capital or assets, or if there are children involved from a previous marriage. If you are going to live in a different state after the wedding, consider having an attorney from that state draw up or review your document.

Nobody likes to talk about divorce or death when planning a wedding, but it is very important to give these issues your utmost consideration. By drawing a prenuptial agreement, you encourage open communication and get a better idea of each other's needs and expectations. You should also consider drawing up or reviewing your wills at this time.

Tips to Save Money: Some software packages allow you to write your own will and prenuptial agreement, which can save you substantial attorney's fees. However, if you decide to draw either agreement on your own, you should still have an attorney review it.

Price Range: $500 - $3,000

BRIDAL GOWN PRESERVATION

The pride and joy you will experience in seeing your daughter and/or granddaughter wear your wedding gown on her wedding day will more than justify the expense of having your gown preserved. Bring your gown to a reputable dry cleaning company which specializes in preserving wedding gowns. They will dry clean your dress, vacuum seal it, and place it in an attractive box. By doing this, your gown will be protected from yellowing, falling apart, or getting damaged over the years. Most boxes have a plastic see-through window where you can show the top part of your dress to friends and family members without having to open the vacuum-sealed container.

Tips to Save Money: Some bridal boutiques offer gown preservation. Try to negotiate having your gown preserved for free with the purchase of a wedding gown. It's well worth the try! But remember, get any agreement in writing and be sure to have it signed by either the owner or the manager of the boutique.

Price Range: $100 - $250

BRIDAL BOUQUET PRESERVATION

The bridal bouquet can be preserved to make a beautiful memento of the wedding.

Things to Consider: Have your bouquet dried, mounted, and framed to hang on your wall or to display on an easel in a quiet corner of your home. You can also have an artist paint your bouquet.

Price Range: $100 - $500

MISCELLANEOUS

WEDDING CONSULTANT

Wedding consultants are professionals whose training, expertise, and contacts will help make your wedding as close to perfect as it can possibly be. They can save you considerable time, money, and stress when planning your wedding. Wedding consultants have information on many ceremony and reception sites as well as reliable service providers, such as photographers, videographers, and florists, which will save you hours of investigation and legwork.

Wedding consultants can provide facilities and service providers to match your budget. They can also save you stress by ensuring that what you are planning is correct and that the service providers you hire are reliable and professional. Most service providers recommended by wedding consultants will go out of their way to do an excellent job for you so that the wedding consultant will continue to recommend their services.

Options: You can have a wedding consultant help you do as much or as little as you think necessary. A consultant can help you plan the whole event from the beginning to the end, helping you formulate a budget, and select your ceremony and reception site, flowers, wedding gown, invitations, and service providers. A wedding consultant can also help you at the end by coordinating the rehearsal and the wedding day. Remember, you want to feel like a guest at your own wedding. You and your family should not have to worry about any details on that special day. This is the wedding consultant's job!

Things to Consider: Strongly consider engaging the services of a wedding consultant. Contrary to what many people believe, a wedding consultant is part of your wedding budget, not an extra expense! A good wedding consultant should be able to save you at least the amount of his/her fee by suggesting less expensive alternatives that still enhance your wedding. In addition, many consultants obtain discounts from the service providers they work with. If this is not enough, they are more than worth their fee by serving as an intermediary between you and your parents and/or service providers.

When hiring a wedding consultant, make sure you check his/her references. Ask the consultant if s/he is a member of the Association of Bridal Consultants (ABC) and ask to see a current membership certificate. All ABC members agree to uphold a Code of Ethics and Standards of Membership. Many consultants have formal training and experience in event planning and in other specialties related to weddings, such as flower arranging and catering.

Price Range: $500 - $10,000

WEDDING PLANNING ONLINE

With a computer and an internet connection, you can ease the process of planning your wedding. A good wedding planning website will help you create a budget, select your service providers, generate a guest list, address invitations and create a wedding timeline. It can also keep track of payments made, invitations sent, RSVPs, gifts received, and much more. You can even create your registry or design a personal web page or website all about your wedding!

Options: WS Publishing Group has a great wedding planning site that follows hand-in-hand with this book! Go to www.WeddingSolutions.com and plan your entire wedding with our online tools.

TAXES

Don't forget to figure in the cost of taxes on all taxable items you purchase for your wedding. Many people make a big mistake by not figuring out the taxes they will have to pay for their wedding expenses. For example, if you are planning a reception for 250 guests with an estimated cost of $60 per person for food and beverages, your pretax expenses would be $15,000. A sales tax of 7.5 percent would mean an additional expense of $1,125! Find out what the sales tax is in your area and which items are taxable and figure this expense into your overall budget.

WEDDING CONSULTANTS COMPARISON CHART

QUESTIONS	POSSIBILITY 1	POSSIBILITY 2
What is the name of the wedding consulting business?		
What is the website and e-mail of the wedding consultant?		
What is the address of the wedding consultant?		
What is the name and phone number of the wedding consultant?		
How many years of professional experience do you have?		
How many consultants are in your company?		
Are you a member of the Association of Bridal Consultants?		
What services do you provide?		
What are your hourly fees?		
What is your fee for complete wedding planning?		
What is your fee to oversee the rehearsal and wedding day?		
What is your payment policy?		
What is your cancellation policy?		
Do you have liability insurance?		

WEDDING CONSULTANTS COMPARISON CHART

POSSIBILITY 3	POSSIBILITY 4	POSSIBILITY 5	POSSIBILITY 6

WEDDING CONSULTANT'S INFORMATION FORM

Make a copy of this form and give it to your wedding consultant.

THE WEDDING OF:

Ceremony Site: _____ Phone Number: _____

Ceremony Address: _____

City: _____ State: _____ Zip Code: _____

Website: _____ E-mail: _____

Reception Site: _____ Phone Number: _____

Reception Address: _____

City: _____ State: _____ Zip Code: _____

Website: _____ E-mail: _____

CEREMONY SERVICES	Contact Person	Arrival Time	Departure Time	Phone Number
Florist				
Musicians				
Officiant				
Photographer				
Rental Supplier				
Site Coordinator				
Soloist				
Transportation				
Videographer				
Other:				

RECEPTION SERVICES	Contact Person	Arrival Time	Departure Time	Phone Number
Baker				
Bartender				
Caterer				
Florist				
Gift Attendant				
Guest Book Attendant				
Musicians				
Rental Supplier				
Site Coordinator				
Transportation				
Valet Service				
Other:				

NAME & ADDRESS CHANGE FORM

TO WHOM IT MAY CONCERN:

This is to inform you of my recent marriage and to request a change of name and/or address. The following information will be effective as of: _____

My account/policy number is: _____

Under the name of: _____

PREVIOUS INFORMATION:

Husband's Name: _____ Phone Number: _____

Previous Address: _____

Wife's Maiden Name: _____ Phone Number: _____

Previous Address: _____

NEW INFORMATION:

Husband's Name: _____ Phone Number: _____

Wife's Name: _____ Phone Number: _____

New Address: _____

SPECIAL INSTRUCTIONS:

❏ Change name

❏ Change address/phone

❏ Add spouse's name

❏ Send necessary forms to include my spouse on my policy/account

❏ We plan to continue service

❏ We plan to discontinue service after: _____

If you have any questions, please feel free to contact us at: (   ) _____

Husband's Signature: _____

Wife's Signature: _____

CHANGE OF ADDRESS WORKSHEET

COMPANY	Account or Policy No.	Phone or Address	Done ✔
Auto Insurance			
Auto Registration			
Bank Accounts			
1)			
2)			
3)			
Credit Cards			
1)			
2)			
3)			
4)			
Dentist			
Doctors			
Driver's License			
Employee Records			
Insurance: Dental			
Insurance: Disability			
Insurance: Homeowner's			
Insurance: Life			
Insurance: Renter's			
Insurance: Other			
IRA Accounts			
1)			
2)			
3)			
Leases			
1)			
2)			
Loan Companies			
1)			
2)			
3)			

CHANGE OF ADDRESS WORKSHEET

COMPANY	Account or Policy No.	Phone or Address	Done ✔
Magazines			
Memberships			
1)			
2)			
3)			
Mortgage			
Newspaper			
1)			
2)			
Passport			
Pensions			
Post Office			
Property Title			
Retirement Accounts			
1)			
2)			
Safe Deposit Box			
School Records			
1)			
2)			
3)			
Social Security			
Stockbroker			
Taxes			
Telephone Company			
Utilities			
Voter Registration			
Will/Trust			
Other:			
Other:			
Other:			
Other:			

NOTES

TIMELINES

THE FOLLOWING SECTION INCLUDES TWO DIFFERENT TIMELINES or schedule of events for your wedding day: one for members of your wedding party and one for the various service providers you have hired. Use these timelines to help your wedding party and service providers understand their roles and where they need to be throughout your wedding day. This will also give you a much better idea of how your special day will unfold.

When preparing your timeline, first list the time that your wedding ceremony will begin. Then work forward or backwards, using the sample as your guide. The samples included give you an idea of how much time each event typically takes. But feel free to change the amount of time allotted for any event when customizing your own.

This is a sample wedding party timeline. To develop your own, use the form on page 228. Use the extra space in the description column to write additional information such as addresses or any other comments that will help members of your wedding party understand what their roles are. Once you have created your own timeline, make a copy and give one to each member of your wedding party.

TIME	DESCRIPTION	BRIDE	BRIDE'S MOTHER	BRIDE'S FATHER	MAID OF HONOR	BRIDESMAIDS	BRIDE'S FAMILY	GROOM	GROOM'S MOTHER	GROOM'S FATHER	BEST MAN	USHERS	GROOM'S FAMILY	FLOWER GIRL	RING BEARER
2:00 PM	Manicurist appointment	✓	✓		✓	✓									
2:30 PM	Hair/makeup appointment	✓	✓		✓	✓									
4:15 PM	Arrive at dressing site	✓	✓		✓	✓									
4:30 PM	Arrive at dressing site							✓			✓	✓			
4:45 PM	Pre-ceremony photos							✓	✓	✓	✓	✓	✓		
5:15 PM	Arrive at ceremony site							✓	✓	✓	✓	✓	✓		
5:15 PM	Pre-ceremony photos	✓	✓	✓	✓	✓	✓								
5:20 PM	Give officiant marriage license and fees										✓				
5:20 PM	Ushers receive seating chart											✓			
5:30 PM	Ushers distribute wedding programs as guests arrive											✓			
5:30 PM	Arrive at ceremony site													✓	✓
5:30 PM	Guest book attendant directs guests to sign book														
5:30 PM	Prelude music begins														
5:35 PM	Ushers begin seating guests											✓			
5:45 PM	Arrive at ceremony site	✓	✓	✓	✓	✓	✓								
5:45 PM	Ushers seat honored guests											✓			
5:50 PM	Ushers seat groom's parents								✓	✓		✓			
5:55 PM	Ushers seat bride's mother		✓									✓			
5:55 PM	Attendants line up for procession				✓	✓						✓		✓	✓
5:56 PM	Bride's father takes his place next to bride	✓		✓											
5:57 PM	Ushers roll out aisle runner											✓			
5:58 PM	Groom's party enters							✓			✓				
6:00 PM	Processional music begins														

WEDDING PARTY TIMELINE (SAMPLE)

TIME	DESCRIPTION	BRIDE	BRIDE'S MOTHER	BRIDE'S FATHER	MAID OF HONOR	BRIDESMAIDS	BRIDE'S FAMILY	GROOM	GROOM'S MOTHER	GROOM'S FATHER	BEST MAN	USHERS	GROOM'S FAMILY	FLOWER GIRL	RING BEARER
6:00 PM	Groom's mother rises								✓						
6:01 PM	Ushers enter											✓			
6:02 PM	Wedding party marches up aisle	✓		✓	✓	✓								✓	✓
6:20 PM	Wedding party marches down aisle	✓			✓			✓			✓			✓	✓
6:22 PM	Parents march down aisle		✓	✓					✓	✓					
6:25 PM	Sign marriage certificate	✓			✓			✓			✓				
6:30 PM	Post-ceremony photos taken	✓	✓	✓	✓	✓	✓	✓	✓	✓	✓	✓	✓	✓	✓
6:30 PM	Cocktails and hors d'oeuvres served														
6:30 PM	Gift attendant watches gifts as guests arrive														
7:15 PM	Band/DJ announces entrance and/or receiving line forms	✓						✓							
7:45 PM	Guests are seated and dinner is served														
8:30 PM	Toasts are given										✓				
8:40 PM	First dance	✓						✓							
8:45 PM	Traditional dances	✓	✓	✓				✓	✓	✓					
9:00 PM	Open dance floor for all guests														
9:30 PM	Bride and groom toast one another before cutting cake	✓						✓							
9:40 PM	Cake-cutting ceremony	✓						✓							
10:00 PM	Bride tosses bouquet to single women	✓			✓	✓								✓	
10:10 PM	Groom removes garter from bride's leg	✓						✓							
10:15 PM	Groom tosses garter to single men							✓			✓	✓			✓
10:20 PM	Man who caught garter places it on bouquet-catching woman's leg														
10:30 PM	Distribute flower petals, rice or birdseed to toss over couple														
10:45 PM	Bride and groom make grand exit	✓						✓							

WEDDING PARTY TIMELINE (CONT.)

Create your own timeline using this form. Make copies and give one to each member of your wedding party.

TIME	DESCRIPTION	BRIDE	BRIDE'S MOTHER	BRIDE'S FATHER	MAID OF HONOR	BRIDESMAIDS	BRIDE'S FAMILY	GROOM	GROOM'S MOTHER	GROOM'S FATHER	BEST MAN	USHERS	GROOM'S FAMILY	FLOWER GIRL	RING BEARER

WEDDING PARTY TIMELINE (CONT.)

Create your own timeline using this form. Make copies and give one to each member of your wedding party.

TIME	DESCRIPTION	BRIDE	BRIDE'S MOTHER	BRIDE'S FATHER	MAID OF HONOR	BRIDESMAIDS	BRIDE'S FAMILY	GROOM	GROOM'S MOTHER	GROOM'S FATHER	BEST MAN	USHERS	GROOM'S FAMILY	FLOWER GIRL	RING BEARER

This is a sample of a service provider timeline. To develop your own, use the form on page 232. Use the extra space in the description column to write additional information such as addresses or any other comments that will help your service providers understand what their roles are and where they should be throughout the day. Once you have created your own timeline, make a copy and give one to each of your service providers.

TIME	DESCRIPTION	BAKERY	CATERER	CEREMONY MUSICIANS	OFFICIANT	OTHER	FLORIST	HAIRSTYLIST	LIMOUSINE	MAKEUP ARTIST	MANICURIST	PARTY RENTALS	PHOTOGRAPHER	RECEPTION MUSICIANS	VIDEOGRAPHER
1:00 PM	Party rental supplier delivers supplies to ceremony site											✓			
1:30 PM	Party rental supplier delivers supplies to reception site											✓			
2:00 PM	Manicurist meets bride at:										✓				
2:30 PM	Makeup artist meets bride at:									✓					
3:00 PM	Hairstylist meets bride at:							✓							
4:00 PM	Limousine picks up bridal party at:								✓						
4:15 PM	Caterer begins setting up		✓												
4:30 PM	Florist arrives at ceremony site						✓								
4:40 PM	Baker delivers cake to reception site	✓													
4:45 PM	Florist arrives at reception site						✓								
4:45 PM	Pre-ceremony photos of groom's family at:												✓		
5:00 PM	Videographer arrives at ceremony site														✓
5:15 PM	Pre-ceremony photos of bride's family at:												✓		
5:20 PM	Ceremony site decorations finalized (guest book, flowers, etc.)					✓	✓								
5:30 PM	Prelude music begins			✓											
5:45 PM	Reception site decorations finalized (gift table, place cards, flowers, etc.)		✓			✓	✓								
5:58 PM	Officiant enters				✓										
6:00 PM	Processional music begins			✓											
6:15 PM	Caterer finishes setting up		✓												
6:25 PM	Sign marriage certificate				✓								✓		✓
6:30 PM	Post-ceremony photos at:												✓		
6:30 PM	Cocktails and hors d'oeuvres served		✓												
6:30 PM	Band or DJ begins playing													✓	

TIME	DESCRIPTION	BAKERY	CATERER	CEREMONY MUSICIANS	OFFICIANT	OTHER	FLORIST	HAIRSTYLIST	LIMOUSINE	MAKEUP ARTIST	MANICURIST	PARTY RENTALS	PHOTOGRAPHER	RECEPTION MUSICIANS	VIDEOGRAPHER
6:30 PM	Transport guest book and gifts to reception site					✓									
6:45 PM	Move arch/urns/flowers to reception site					✓									
7:00 PM	Limousine picks up bride and groom at ceremony site								✓						
7:15 PM	Band/DJ announces entrance of bride and groom													✓	
7:45 PM	Dinner is served		✓												
8:15 PM	Champagne served for toasts		✓												
8:30 PM	Band/DJ announces toast by best man													✓	
8:40 PM	Band/DJ announces first dance													✓	
9:00 PM	Transport gifts to:					✓									
9:30 PM	Band/DJ announces cake-cutting ceremony													✓	
10:30 PM	Transport top tier of cake, cake-top, flowers, etc. to:					✓									
10:40 PM	Transport rental items to:					✓									
10:45 PM	Limousine picks up bride and groom at reception site								✓						
11:00 PM	Videographer departs														✓
11:00 PM	Photographer departs												✓		
11:00 PM	Wedding consultant departs					✓									
11:30 PM	Band/DJ stops playing													✓	
11:45 PM	Party rental supplier picks up supplies at ceremony/reception sites											✓			

SERVICE PROVIDER TIMELINE (CONT.)

Create your own timeline using this form. Make copies and give one to each of your service providers.

TIME	DESCRIPTION	BAKERY	CATERER	CEREMONY MUSICIANS	OFFICIANT	OTHER	FLORIST	HAIRSTYLIST	LIMOUSINE	MAKEUP ARTIST	MANICURIST	PARTY RENTALS	PHOTOGRAPHER	RECEPTION MUSICIANS	VIDEOGRAPHER

SERVICE PROVIDER TIMELINE (CONT.)

Create your own timeline using this form. Make copies and give one to each of your service providers.

TIME	DESCRIPTION	BAKERY	CATERER	CEREMONY MUSICIANS	OFFICIANT	OTHER	FLORIST	HAIRSTYLIST	LIMOUSINE	MAKEUP ARTIST	MANICURIST	PARTY RENTALS	PHOTOGRAPHER	RECEPTION MUSICIANS	VIDEOGRAPHER

NOTES

WEDDING TRADITIONS

HAVE YOU EVER WONDERED WHY CERTAIN THINGS are almost always done at weddings? For example, why does the bride carry a bouquet or wear a veil? Or why do guests throw rice or rose petals over the newlyweds? In this section we discuss the origin and symbolism of some of the most popular wedding traditions.

THE BRIDE'S BOUQUET

In history, a bride carried her bouquet for protective reasons—carrying strong-smelling spices or garlic could help to drive away evil spirits which might plague the wedding. Eventually the floral bouquet became prevalent and symbolized fertility and the hope for a large family. Each flower was assigned a particular meaning when carried in a bride's bouquet.

THE BRIDE'S VEIL

The veil has historically symbolized virginity and innocence. It is believed that, in ancient times, a bride was veiled to protect her from evil spirits or to shield her from her husband's eyes. Arranged marriages were common and often they were not to officially meet until AFTER the wedding.

WEDDING TRADITIONS

RICE AND PETALS

The tossing of rice began to aid with fertility, both for the couple and for their harvest.

SOMETHING OLD, SOMETHING NEW, SOMETHING BORROWED, SOMETHING BLUE

Something old is carried to represent the history of the bride and ties her to her family. Something new represents the future and the bride's ties to her new family. Something borrowed should come from someone who is happily married and is carried in the hopes that their good fortune may rub off on you. Blue is the color of purity and is carried to represent faithfulness in the marriage. Many people don't realize that there is one more item—a sixpence in your shoe—which represents wealth.

WHITE AISLE RUNNER

Using a white aisle runner symbolizes bringing God into your union and is indicative of walking on holy ground.

SPECIAL SEATING FOR THE FAMILIES

The families are traditionally seated on opposite sides of the church, because in ancient times families would often have a wedding in order to bring peace to warring clans. In order to prevent fighting from taking place during the wedding, they were kept separate.

THE GROOM ENTERING FIRST

Traditionally, the groom enters first and gives his vows first, because he is considered to be the one who has initiated the wedding.

THE FATHER OF THE BRIDE WALKING DOWN THE AISLE

In historic times, brides were literally given away by their fathers—women were betrothed, often at birth, to men they did not know, and their parents were able to "give them away." Now, giving the bride away is simply a way for the bride's family to publicly show their support of the union.

THE BRIDE STANDING ON THE LEFT

Because ancient times were so violent and unpredictable, a bride was likely to be kidnapped and held for ransom at her wedding! The bride was placed on the groom's left in order to leave his sword-hand free in case he had to defend her.

THE SYMBOLISM OF THE WEDDING RINGS

The circle of the wedding ring represents eternal love and devotion. The Greeks believed that the fourth finger on the left hand has a vein which leads directly to the heart, so this is the finger onto which we place these bands.

KISSING THE BRIDE

During the Roman empire, the kiss between a couple symbolized a legal bond—hence the expression "sealed with a kiss." Continued use of the kiss to seal the marriage bond is based on the deeply rooted idea of the kiss as a vehicle for transference of power and souls.

THE COUPLE BEING PRONOUNCED "HUSBAND AND WIFE"

This establishes their change of names and a definite point in time for the beginning of the marriage. These words are to remove any doubt in the minds of the couple or the witnesses concerning the validity of the marriage.

SIGNING THE WEDDING PAPERS

The newlywed couple signs the wedding papers to establish a public document and a continuing public record of the covenant.

SIGNING THE GUEST BOOK

Your wedding guests are official witnesses to the covenant. By signing the guest book, they are saying, "I have witnessed the vows, and I will testify to the reality of this marriage." Because of this significance, the guest book should be signed after the wedding rather than before it.

WEDDING TRADITIONS

THE PURPOSE OF THE RECEIVING LINE

The receiving line is for guests to give their blessings to the couple and their parents.

THE BRIDE AND GROOM FEEDING WEDDING CAKE TO EACH OTHER

This represents the sharing of their body to become one. A New Testament illustration of this symbolism is The Lord's Supper.

DO'S & DON'TS

YOUR WEDDING WILL LAST ONLY A FEW HOURS but will likely take several months to plan. That is why it is so important to enjoy the complete wedding planning process. This is a time to get excited, to fall even more deeply in love with each other, to learn more about each other, and to compromise. If you can handle planning your wedding with your fiancé and parents, you can handle anything! Here is a list of do's and don'ts to follow when planning your special day. If you follow these suggestions, your wedding planning and your wedding day will be much more enjoyable!

DO'S

- Hire a professional wedding consultant.

- Maintain a sense of humor.

- Maintain open communication with your fiancé and with both sets of parents, especially if they are financing the wedding.

- Be receptive to your parents' ideas, especially if they are financing the wedding.

- Be flexible and keep your overall budget in mind.

- Maintain a regular routine of exercise and eat a well-balanced diet.

- Buy *The Ultimate Groom's Guide*, published by Wedding Solutions Publishing, and give it to your fiancé.

- Buy the *Wedding Party Responsibility Cards*, published by Wedding Solutions Publishing, and give a card to each member of your wedding party.

- Register for gifts; consider a price range that your guests can afford.

- Break in your shoes well before your wedding day.

- Practice with makeup and various hairstyles for your wedding day.

DO'S & DON'TS

DO'S

• Check recent references for all of your service providers.

• Get everything in writing with your service providers.

• Assign your guests to tables and group them together by age, interests, acquaintances, etc.

• Consider drawing up a prenuptial agreement and a will.

• Send thank-you notes as soon as you receive gifts.

• Give a rose to each of your mothers as you walk down the aisle during the recessional.

• Try to spend some time with each of your guests and personally thank them for coming to your wedding.

• Encourage the bride's parents to introduce their family and friends to the family and friends of the groom's family, and vice versa.

• Toast both sets of parents at the rehearsal dinner and/or at the reception. Thank them for everything they have done for you and for giving you a beautiful wedding.

• Eat well at the reception, especially if you will be drinking alcohol.

• Keep a smile on your face; there will be many photographs taken of both of you.

• Expect things to go wrong on your wedding day. Most likely if something does go wrong, no one will notice it but yourself. Relax and don't let it bother you.

• Preserve the top tier of your wedding cake for your first year anniversary.

• Send a special gift to both sets of parents, such as a small album containing the best photographs of the wedding. Personalize this gift by having it engraved with your names and the date of your wedding.

DON'TS

- Don't get involved in other activities; you will be very busy planning your wedding.

- Don't make any major decisions without discussing it openly with your fiancé.

- Don't be controlling. Be open to other people's ideas.

- Don't overspend your budget; this can be extremely stressful.

- Don't wait until the last minute to hire your service providers. The good ones get booked months in advance.

- Don't try to make everyone happy; it is impossible and will only make your wedding planning more difficult.

- Don't try to impress your friends.

- Don't invite old boyfriends or girlfriends to your wedding, unless both you and your fiancé are friendly with them; you don't want to make anybody uncomfortable.

- Don't try to do "everything." Delegate responsibilities to your fiancé, your parents, and to members of your wedding party.

- Don't rely on friends or family to photograph or videotape your wedding. Hire professionals!

- Don't assume that members of your wedding party know what to do. Give them direction with your Wedding Party Timeline and the *Wedding Party Responsibility Cards*, available at most major bookstores.

- Don't assume your service providers know what to do. Give each of them a copy of your detailed Service Provider Timeline.

- Don't schedule your bachelor party the night before the wedding. You don't want to have a hangover on your special day!

- Don't arrive late to the ceremony!

- Don't drink too much during the reception; you don't want to make a fool of yourself on your most special day!

- Don't flirt with members of the opposite sex.

DO'S & DON'TS

DON'TS

• Don't allow your guests to drive drunk after the reception; you may be held responsible.

• Don't rub cake in the face of your spouse during the cake-cutting ceremony; your spouse might not appreciate it!

• Don't overeat; this may upset your stomach or make you sleepy.

• Don't leave your reception without saying good-bye to your family and friends.

• Don't drive if you have had too much to drink!

WEDDING PARTY RESPONSIBILITIES

EACH MEMBER OF YOUR WEDDING PARTY has his/her own individual duties and responsibilities. The following is a list of the most important duties for each member of your wedding party.

The most convenient method for conveying this information to members of your wedding party is by purchasing a set of the *Wedding Party Responsibility Cards*, published by WS Publishing Group.

These cards are attractive and contain all the information your wedding party needs to know to assure a smooth wedding: what to do, how to do it, when to do it, when to arrive, and much more. They also include financial responsibilities as well as the processional, recessional, and altar lineup.

This book is available at most major bookstores.

WEDDING PARTY RESPONSIBILITIES

MAID OF HONOR

- Helps bride select attire and address invitations.
- Plans bridal shower.
- Arrives at dressing site two hours before ceremony to assist bride in dressing.
- Arrives dressed at ceremony site one hour before the wedding for photographs.
- Arranges the bride's veil and train before the processional and recessional.
- Holds bride's bouquet and groom's ring, if no ring bearer, during the ceremony.
- Witnesses the signing of the marriage license.
- Keeps bride on schedule.
- Dances with best man during the bridal party dance.
- Helps bride change into her going away clothes.
- Mails wedding announcements after the wedding.
- Returns bridal slip, if rented.

BEST MAN

- Responsible for organizing ushers' activities.
- Organizes bachelor party for groom.
- Drives groom to ceremony site and sees that he is properly dressed before the wedding.
- Arrives dressed at ceremony site one hour before the wedding for photographs.
- Brings marriage license to wedding.
- Pays the clergyman, musicians, photographer, and any other service providers the day of the wedding.
- Holds the bride's ring for the groom, if no ring bearer, until needed by officiant.
- Witnesses the signing of the marriage license.
- Drives newlyweds to reception, if no hired driver.
- Offers first toast at reception, usually before dinner.
- Keeps groom on schedule.
- Dances with maid of honor during the bridal party dance.
- May drive couple to airport or honeymoon suite.
- Oversees return of tuxedo rentals for groom and ushers, on time and in good condition.

BRIDESMAIDS

- Assist maid of honor in planning bridal shower.
- Assist bride with errands and addressing invitations.
- Participate in all pre-wedding parties.
- Arrive at dressing site two hours before ceremony.
- Arrive dressed at ceremony site one hour before the wedding for photographs.

- Walk behind ushers in order of height during the processional, either in pairs or in single file.
- Sit next to ushers at the head table.
- Dance with ushers and other important guests.
- Encourage single women to participate in the bouquet-tossing ceremony.

USHERS

- Help best man with bachelor party.
- Arrive dressed at ceremony site one hour before the wedding for photographs.
- Distribute wedding programs and maps to the reception as guests arrive.
- Seat guests at the ceremony as follows:
    - If female, offer the right arm.
    - If male, walk along his left side.
    - If couple, offer right arm to female; male follows a step or two behind.
    - Seat bride's guests in left pews.
    - Seat groom's guests in right pews.
    - Maintain equal number of guests in left and right pews, if possible.
    - If a group of guests arrive at the same time, seat the eldest woman first.
    - Just prior to the processional, escort groom's mother to her seat; then escort bride's mother to her seat.
- Two ushers may roll carpet down the aisle after both mothers are seated.
- If pew ribbons are used, two ushers may loosen them one row at a time after the ceremony.
- Direct guests to the reception site.
- Dance with bridesmaids and other important guests.

BRIDE'S MOTHER

- Helps prepare guest list for bride and her family.
- Helps plan the wedding ceremony and reception.
- Helps bride select her bridal gown.
- Helps bride keep track of gifts received.
- Selects her own attire according to the formality and color of the wedding.
- Makes accommodations for bride's out-of-town guests.
- Arrives dressed at ceremony site one hour before the wedding for photographs.
- Is the last person to be seated right before the processional begins.
- Sits in the left front pew to the left of bride's father during the ceremony.
- May stand up to signal the start of the processional.
- Can witness the signing of the marriage license.
- Dances with the groom after the first dance.
- Acts as hostess at the reception.

WEDDING PARTY RESPONSIBILITIES

BRIDE'S FATHER

- Helps prepare guest list for bride and her family.
- Selects attire that complements groom's attire.
- Rides to the ceremony with bride in limousine.
- Arrives dressed at ceremony site one hour before the wedding for photographs.
- After giving bride away, sits in the left front pew to the right of bride's mother. If divorced, sits in second or third row unless financing the wedding.
- When officiant asks, "Who gives this bride away?" answers, "Her mother and I do," or something similar.
- Can witness the signing of the marriage license.
- Dances with bride after first dance.
- Acts as host at the reception.

GROOM'S MOTHER

- Helps prepare guest list for groom and his family.
- Selects attire that complements mother of the bride's attire.
- Makes accommodations for groom's out-of-town guests.
- With groom's father, plans rehearsal dinner.
- Arrives dressed at ceremony site one hour before the wedding for photographs.
- May stand up to signal the start of the processional.
- Can witness the signing of the marriage license.

GROOM'S FATHER

- Helps prepare guest list for groom and his family.
- Selects attire that complements groom's attire.
- With groom's mother, plans rehearsal dinner.
- Offers toast to bride at rehearsal dinner.
- Arrives dressed at ceremony site one hour before the wedding for photographs.
- Can witness the signing of the marriage license.

FLOWER GIRL

- Usually between the ages of four and eight.
- Attends rehearsal to practice, but is not required to attend pre-wedding parties.
- Arrives dressed at ceremony site 45 minutes before the wedding for photos.

- Carries a basket filled with loose rose petals to strew along bride's path during processional, if allowed by ceremony site.
- If very young, may sit with her parents during ceremony.

RING BEARER

- Usually between the ages of four and eight.
- Attends rehearsal to practice but is not required to attend pre-wedding parties.
- Arrives at ceremony site 45 minutes before the wedding for photographs.
- Carries a white pillow with rings attached.
- If younger than seven years, carries mock rings.
- If very young, may sit with his parents during ceremony.
- If mock rings are used, turns the ring pillow over at the end of the ceremony.

WEDDING PARTY FORM

Make a copy of this form and give it to your wedding consultant.

PARENTS	Name	Responsibilities	Phone #1	Phone #2
Bride's Mother				
Bride's Father				
Groom's Mother				
Groom's Father				

BRIDE'S ATTENDANTS	Name	Responsibilities	Phone #1	Phone #2
Maid of Honor				
Matron of Honor				
Bridesmaid #1				
Bridesmaid #2				
Bridesmaid #3				
Bridesmaid #4				
Bridesmaid #5				
Bridesmaid #6				
Flower Girl				
Other:				

GROOM'S ATTENDANTS	Name	Responsibilities	Phone #1	Phone #2
Best Man				
Usher #1				
Usher #2				
Usher #3				
Usher #4				
Usher #5				
Usher #6				
Ring Bearer				
Other:				

WHO PAYS FOR WHAT

BRIDE AND/OR BRIDE'S FAMILY

- Engagement party
- Wedding consultant's fee
- Bridal gown, veil, and accessories
- Wedding stationery, calligraphy, and postage
- Wedding gift for bridal couple
- Groom's wedding ring
- Gifts for bridesmaids
- Bridesmaids' bouquets
- Pre-wedding parties and bridesmaids' luncheon
- Photography and videography
- Bride's medical exam and blood test
- Wedding guest book and other accessories
- Total cost of the ceremony, including location, flowers, music, rental items, and accessories
- Total cost of the reception, including location, flowers, music, rental items, accessories, food, beverages, cake, decorations, favors, etc.
- Transportation for bridal party to ceremony and reception
- Own attire and travel expenses

GROOM AND/OR GROOM'S FAMILY

- Own travel expenses and attire
- Rehearsal dinner
- Wedding gift for bridal couple
- Bride's wedding ring
- Gifts for groom's attendants
- Medical exam for groom including blood test
- Bride's bouquet and going away corsage
- Mothers' and grandmothers' corsages
- All boutonnieres
- Officiant's fee
- Marriage license
- Honeymoon expenses

WHO PAYS FOR WHAT

ATTENDANTS

- Own attire except flowers
- Travel expenses
- Bridal shower paid for by maid of honor and bridesmaids
- Bachelor party paid for by best man and ushers

WEDDING FORMATIONS

THE FOLLOWING SECTION ILLUSTRATES THE TYPICAL CEREMONY FORMATIONS (processional, recessional, and altar lineup) for both Christian and Jewish weddings, as well as the typical formations for the receiving line, head table, and parents' tables at the reception.

These ceremony formations are included in the *Wedding Party Responsibility Cards*, published by WS Publishing Group. This attractive set of cards makes it very easy for members of your wedding party to remember their place in these formations. Give one card to each member of your wedding party ... they will appreciate it. This book of cards is available at most major bookstores.

$\mathscr{A}$LTAR $\mathscr{L}$INE $\mathscr{U}$P

Bride's Pews   Groom's Pews

ABBREVIATIONS

B=Bride	GF=Groom's Father	G=Groom	GM=Groom's Mother
BM=Best Man	BMa=Bridesmaids	MH=Maid of Honor	U=Ushers
BF=Bride's Father	FG=Flower Girl	BMo=Bride's Mother	RB=Ring Bearer
O=Officiant			

*P*ROCESSIONAL *R*ECESSIONAL

ABBREVIATIONS

B=Bride	GF=Groom's Father	G=Groom	GM=Groom's Mother
BM=Best Man	BMa=Bridesmaids	MH=Maid of Honor	U=Ushers
BF=Bride's Father	FG=Flower Girl	BMo=Bride's Mother	RB=Ring Bearer
O=Officiant			

*A*LTAR *L*INE *U*P

Groom's Pews   Bride's Pews

ABBREVIATIONS

B=Bride   GF=Groom's Father   G=Groom   GM=Groom's Mother
BM=Best Man   BMa=Bridesmaids   MH=Maid of Honor   U=Ushers
BF=Bride's Father   FG=Flower Girl   BMo=Bride's Mother   RB=Ring Bearer
R=Rabbi

*P*ROCESSIONAL   *R*ECESSIONAL

ABBREVIATIONS

B=Bride	GF=Groom's Father
BM=Best Man	BMa=Bridesmaids
BF=Bride's Father	FG=Flower Girl
R=Rabbi	

G=Groom	GM=Groom's Mother
MH=Maid of Honor	U=Ushers
BMo=Bride's Mother	RB=Ring Bearer

Receiving Line

Head Table

Parents' Table

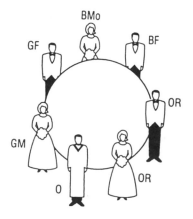

ABBREVIATIONS

B=Bride	GF=Groom's Father	G=Groom	GM=Groom's Mother
BM=Best Man	BMa=Bridesmaids	MH=Maid of Honor	U=Ushers
BF=Bride's Father	OR=Other Relatives	BMo=Bride's Mother	O=Officiant

THINGS TO BRING

TO THE REHEARSAL

BRIDE'S LIST

- ❏ Wedding announcements (give to maid of honor to mail after wedding)
- ❏ Bridesmaids' gifts (if not already given)
- ❏ Camera and film
- ❏ Fake bouquet or ribbon bouquet from bridal shower
- ❏ Groom's gift (if not already given)
- ❏ Reception maps and wedding programs
- ❏ Rehearsal information and ceremony formations
- ❏ Flower girl basket and ring bearer pillow
- ❏ Seating diagrams for head table and parents' tables
- ❏ Wedding schedule of events/timeline
- ❏ Tape/CD player with wedding music

GROOM'S LIST

- ❏ Bride's gift (if not already given)
- ❏ Marriage license
- ❏ Ushers' gifts (if not already given)
- ❏ Service providers' fees to give to best man or wedding consultant so s/he can pay them at the wedding

THINGS TO BRING

TO THE CEREMONY

BRIDE'S LIST
- ❑ Aspirin/Alka Seltzer
- ❑ Bobby pins
- ❑ Breath spray/mints
- ❑ Bridal gown
- ❑ Bridal gown box
- ❑ Cake knife
- ❑ Going away clothes
- ❑ Clear nail polish
- ❑ Deodorant
- ❑ Garter
- ❑ Gloves
- ❑ Groom's ring
- ❑ Guest book
- ❑ Hairbrush
- ❑ Hair spray

- ❑ Headpiece
- ❑ Iron
- ❑ Jewelry
- ❑ Kleenex
- ❑ Lint brush
- ❑ Luggage
- ❑ Makeup
- ❑ Mirror
- ❑ Nail polish
- ❑ Panty hose
- ❑ Passport
- ❑ Perfume
- ❑ Personal camera
- ❑ Plume pen for guest book
- ❑ Powder

- ❑ Purse
- ❑ Safety pins
- ❑ Scotch tape/masking tape
- ❑ Sewing kit
- ❑ Shoes
- ❑ Something old
- ❑ Something new
- ❑ Something borrowed
- ❑ Something blue
- ❑ Sixpence for shoe
- ❑ Spot remover
- ❑ Straight pins
- ❑ Tampons or sanitary napkins
- ❑ Toasting goblets
- ❑ Toothbrush and paste

GROOM'S LIST
- ❑ Airline tickets
- ❑ Announcements
- ❑ Aspirin/Alka Seltzer
- ❑ Breath spray/mints
- ❑ Bride's ring
- ❑ Going away clothes
- ❑ Cologne
- ❑ Cuff Links

- ❑ Cummerbund
- ❑ Deodorant
- ❑ Hair comb
- ❑ Hair product
- ❑ Kleenex
- ❑ Lint brush
- ❑ Luggage
- ❑ Neck tie

- ❑ Passport
- ❑ Shirt
- ❑ Shoes
- ❑ Socks
- ❑ Toothbrush and paste
- ❑ Tuxedo
- ❑ Underwear

WEDDING PLANNING CALENDAR

THE NEXT SEVERAL MONTHS WILL BE FILLED WITH IMPORTANT DATES. Make sure you allow yourself adequate time to book your ceremony and reception site in advance, schedule meetings with caters, photographers, florists, and bakeries—and still have time to take care of any other wedding planning details.

Use the 12-month calendar on the following pages to document your wedding date, parties, all of your appointments, scheduled payments, and any other items you want to complete by a certain date.

If you are planning on a health, fitness, and/or beauty regime during your wedding planning process, write down your routine on this calendar to keep you on track and help you reach your goal.

How to use the calendar: Assign the last calendar page provided for the month your wedding will take place. Then work backwards and simply fill in the month, year, and number of months before your wedding at the top of each page. Then fill in the dates based on each month.

WEDDING PLANNING CALENDAR

Month:_____   20_____   Number of months before wedding:_____

Sunday	Monday	Tuesday	Wednesday	Thursday	Friday	Saturday
☐	☐	☐	☐	☐	☐	☐
☐	☐	☐	☐	☐	☐	☐
☐	☐	☐	☐	☐	☐	☐
☐	☐	☐	☐	☐	☐	☐
☐	☐	☐	☐	☐	☐	☐

Notes:_____

_____

WEDDING PLANNING CALENDAR

Month:_____ 20_____ Number of months before wedding:_____

Sunday	Monday	Tuesday	Wednesday	Thursday	Friday	Saturday
☐	☐	☐	☐	☐	☐	☐
☐	☐	☐	☐	☐	☐	☐
☐	☐	☐	☐	☐	☐	☐
☐	☐	☐	☐	☐	☐	☐
☐	☐	☐	☐	☐	☐	☐

Notes:_____

WEDDING PLANNING CALENDAR

Month:_____ 20_____ Number of months before wedding:_____

Sunday	Monday	Tuesday	Wednesday	Thursday	Friday	Saturday

Notes:_____

_____

WEDDING PLANNING CALENDAR

Month:_____ 20_____ Number of months before wedding:_____

Sunday	Monday	Tuesday	Wednesday	Thursday	Friday	Saturday

Notes:_____

WEDDING PLANNING CALENDAR

Month:_____ 20_____ Number of months before wedding:_____

Sunday	Monday	Tuesday	Wednesday	Thursday	Friday	Saturday
☐	☐	☐	☐	☐	☐	☐
☐	☐	☐	☐	☐	☐	☐
☐	☐	☐	☐	☐	☐	☐
☐	☐	☐	☐	☐	☐	☐
☐	☐	☐	☐	☐	☐	☐

Notes:_____

_____

Month:_____ 20_____ Number of months before wedding:_____

Sunday	Monday	Tuesday	Wednesday	Thursday	Friday	Saturday

Notes:_____

_____

WEDDING PLANNING CALENDAR

Month:_____   20_____   Number of months before wedding:_____

Sunday	Monday	Tuesday	Wednesday	Thursday	Friday	Saturday

Notes:_____

_____

Month:_____   20_____   Number of months before wedding:_____

Sunday	Monday	Tuesday	Wednesday	Thursday	Friday	Saturday

Notes:_____

_____

WEDDING PLANNING CALENDAR

Month:_____ 20_____ Number of months before wedding:_____

Sunday	Monday	Tuesday	Wednesday	Thursday	Friday	Saturday

Notes:_____

Month:_____ 20_____ Number of months before wedding:_____

Sunday	Monday	Tuesday	Wednesday	Thursday	Friday	Saturday
☐	☐	☐	☐	☐	☐	☐
☐	☐	☐	☐	☐	☐	☐
☐	☐	☐	☐	☐	☐	☐
☐	☐	☐	☐	☐	☐	☐
☐	☐	☐	☐	☐	☐	☐

Notes:_____

_____

WEDDING PLANNING CALENDAR

Month:_____   20_____   Number of months before wedding:_____

Sunday	Monday	Tuesday	Wednesday	Thursday	Friday	Saturday

Notes:_____

_____

Month:_____ 20_____ Number of months before wedding:_____

Sunday	Monday	Tuesday	Wednesday	Thursday	Friday	Saturday

Notes:_____
_____

DATES TO REMEMBER

"At the touch of love everyone
becomes a poet."
~ Plato

HONEYMOONS 275

TYPES OF HONEYMOONS 276

CHOOSING YOUR DESTINATION 279

CREATING A WISH LIST 280

HELPFUL RESOURCES 287

TRAVEL AGENTS 287

SOURCES TO READ 290

STATE TOURISM BUREAUS 292

INTERNATIONAL TOURISM BUREAUS 293

OTHER TOURISM BUREAUS AND SERVICES 296

CREATING A BUDGET 297

TIPPING GUIDE 307

THINGS TO PACK 309

PACKING CHECKLIST 310

INTERNATIONAL TRAVEL 315

PASSPORTS AND VISAS 315

UNITED STATES PASSPORT AGENCIES 317

HEALTH CONCERNS 318

OTHER CONCERNS 319

HONEYMOON PLANNER

EASY HONEYMOON PLANNING

A comprehensive guide containing all the information a bride
and groom should know when planning a honeymoon.

HONEYMOONS

YOUR HONEYMOON IS THE TIME TO CELEBRATE YOUR NEW LIFE together as a married couple. It should be the vacation of a lifetime. This does not necessarily mean spending your life's earnings, but the vacation should reflect the special interests you share as a couple.

The honeymoon is traditionally the groom's responsibility. However, the planning of your honeymoon should be a joint decision as to where to go, how long to stay, and how much money to spend.

You will find many tools and suggestions on the following pages to help you plan this important trip. After reading this book, you will have information on different types of honeymoons, and you should be able to determine the perfect honeymoon destination, research and select a responsible travel agent, gather useful information using the resource leads provided, establish a reasonable budget with confidence, and—most importantly—walk away with the assurance that you are planning the honeymoon of a lifetime! Start planning your honeymoon months before the wedding. Many locations that are popular with honeymooners tend to book fairly quickly, so the earlier you plan your trip, the better values you'll usually find.

There are many choices to make and many plans to be made, but most of them seem to fall into place once you've made the toughest decision ... where to go.

Many people have a preconceived notion of where a honeymoon should take place. Indeed, year after year these locations are some of the places most frequently visited by newlyweds. We'll take a look at some of these "traditional" destinations as well as some that are a little less traditional.

Think about what you and your fiancé might find appealing (and unappealing) in the following honeymoon vacations. Be careful not to assume what your new spouse may be looking for in a honeymoon. Couples are often surprised when they discover what the other partner considers a "vacation." Refer to the section entitled Choosing a Destination to determine what each other's ideal vacation includes.

HONEYMOONS

TYPES OF HONEYMOONS

Listed on the following pages are sample honeymoon plans—both traditional and less traditional. A brief description of some of the most popular honeymoon trips (ones that have remained popular with newlyweds for generations) is provided as well.

You can get very helpful information on planning a vacation package in the following brochures from the United States Tour Operator Association, (212) 599-6599, www.ustoa.com.

- *How to Select a Tour Vacation Package*
- *Worldwide Tour and Vacation Package Finder*
- *The Standard for Confident Travel*

TRADITIONAL HONEYMOONS

CRUISES

Cruises are a popular retreat for those who want the luxury of a hospitable resort with the added benefit of visiting one or more new areas. There are hundreds of different cruise options available to you. Typically, almost everything is included in the cost of your cruise: extravagant dining, unlimited group and individual activities, relaxing days and lively nights.

Costs vary greatly depending on the location the cruise will visit (if any) and your cabin accommodations. Locations range from traveling the Mississippi River to circling the Greek Isles. Spend some time choosing your cabin. Most of them are small, but pay attention to distracting things, such as noisy areas and busy pathways, that might be located close by.

Even though most everything is included in your cost, be sure to ask about those items which may not be included. Alcoholic beverages, sundries, spa treatments and tips generally are not included. Request a helpful publication entitled *Answers to Your Most Frequently Asked Questions*, published by Cruise Lines International Association, (212) 921-0066, www.cruising.org.

ALL-INCLUSIVE RESORTS

Many newlyweds, tired from the previous months of wedding planning and accompanying stress, opt for the worry-free guarantee of an all-inclusive resort. Some resorts are for the entire family, some are for couples only (not necessarily newlywed), and some are strictly for honeymooners. Most of these resorts are nestled on a picturesque island beach catering to your relaxation needs.

Most offer numerous sports, water activities, entertainment, and exceptional service and attention. Your costs will vary depending on the location you choose, and there are many to choose from. "All-inclusive" means everything is included in your price. You won't have to worry about meals, drinks, tour fees or even tips.

One way of considering if this is a good option for you is to list all of the activities that the vacation package offers that you are interested in. Add up the individual costs and compare. If you wouldn't be participating much in the activities, food, and drink, you may actually save money by arranging your own trip at an independent resort. Even still, many couples prefer to spend the extra money in exchange for a vacation free of planning and wearying decisions.

Because of its convenience, many couples choose this resort option as the setting for their honeymoon. Some of the most popular all-inclusive resorts are Sandals and Club Med.

THE POCONOS

The Poconos Honeymoon resorts are located in Pennsylvania and are considered to be some of the most popular Honeymoon destinations around. The Poconos offer a variety of individual resorts, each heavily laden with fanciful symbols of romance and sweet desires. The atmosphere is perfect for those who want to be enveloped in a surrounding where you'll never forget you're in love and on your honeymoon. Some travel packages here are considered all-inclusive, but as always, be sure to ask about exclusions and extras. For information about honeymooning in the Poconos, call 1 - 800 - POCONOS.

WALT DISNEY WORLD

Another popular destination for those seeking a "theme" resort are those offered as Disney's Fairy Tale Honeymoons. These vacation packages include accommodations at Disney's exclusive resorts and admission to their theme parks. Some packages are also available with accommodations at some of the privately owned resorts at Disney World. Prices for Disney packages can range greatly depending on your tastes and the amount of activity you desire. For information on Disney's honeymoon packages, call (407) 828-3400 or visit them online at www.disneyweddings.com.

Inquire with your travel agent about day or overnight cruises leaving from nearby ports in Florida. This is one way to combine two very popular honeymoon options into one!

HONEYMOONS

OTHER POPULAR AND TRADITIONAL HONEYMOON PLANS ARE AS FOLLOWS

- Enjoying the beaches and unique treasures of the Hawaiian islands

- Exploring Northern California's romantic wine country

- Ski and snowboard package getaways in Vermont, New Hampshire, Colorado, and Northern California

- Camping and hiking within the beautiful and adventurous National Parks

- Sightseeing, touring, and exploring a variety of points in Europe via the rail system

- Island hopping on a cruise ship around the Greek Isles

- Enjoying a fanciful and adventurous journey on the Orient Express

LESS TRADITIONAL HONEYMOONS

- Bicycling in Nova Scotia while relaxing at quaint bed and breakfast inns

- Participating in a white water river rafting expedition

- Mingling with the owners and fellow guests on an Old West dude ranch

- Visiting landmarks and parks while enjoying the convenience of a traveling home in a rented RV

- Mustering up the courage and stamina for an aggressive hiking tour of the Canadian Rockies

- Training for and participating in a dog sled race in the brisk tundra of Alaska

- "Roughing it" while enjoying the splendor of a safari in East Africa

CHOOSING YOUR DESTINATION

MAYBE YOUR IDEA OF A PERFECT HONEYMOON is ten days of adventure and discovery; but for your fiancé, it may be ten days of resting in a beach chair and romantic strolls in the evening. The choices for honeymoon vacations are as varied as the bride and groom themselves. Deciding together on a honeymoon destination is a wonderful opportunity to discover more about each other and negotiate a vacation that will leave both of you relaxed, fulfilled, and even more in love.

First, determine the type of atmosphere and climate you prefer. Then consider the types of activities you would like to engage in.

Do you want the weather to be hot for swimming at the beach ... or warm for long guided tours of unknown cities ... or cooler for daylong hikes in the woods ... or cold for optimum skiing conditions? Keep in mind the time of year in which your wedding falls. Will you be escaping from extreme temperatures?

If you have a specific destination in mind, you (or your travel agent) will need to do some research to be sure the weather conditions will be suitable for your planned activities.

Review the previous chapters on traditional and nontraditional honeymoons and note what you feel are the pros and cons of each type of vacation. The two of you should have lots of images and possibilities in your mind at this point! The next step is to determine the most perfect atmosphere to provide the setting for your honeymoon. The following sections, "Creating a Wish List" and "Helpful Resources," will guide you through this next step and beyond.

CHOOSING YOUR DESTINATION

CREATING A WISH LIST

Together with your fiancé, complete the wish list worksheet on pages 283 through 285. You should each check off your preferences, even if both of you don't agree on them. There are many locations that provide a variety of activities. Remember, you don't need to spend every minute of your honeymoon together, but your honeymoon destination should be one that intrigues both of you.

This worksheet is divided into 5 sections. You will be considering location, accommodations, meals, activities, and nightlife. While completing the worksheet, be as true to your interests as possible; don't concern yourself with finances and practicality at this point. This is your chance to let your mind wander! Think about what you would like to fill your days and nights with. This is the honeymoon of your dreams.

You step out of the plane, train, car or boat that took you to your honeymoon destination. You sigh with satisfaction at the memory of your flawless and enjoyable wedding as your feet touch the ground.

What type of overall atmosphere do you see yourself stepping into? What is the weather like?

Do you picture a long stretch of beach, towering mountains, blossoming vineyards, or city skyscrapers? Is the dry sand of the desert blowing, or is everything captured under glistening snow caps?

Are there many people walking around (many locals, many tourists), or is it a secluded retreat?

Are you relaxing indoors in a resort with a pampering environment that caters to your comfort, or do you return to a simple, modest hotel or motel after a long day of sightseeing, touring, and dining? Are you camping in the middle of your activities—hiking, climbing, fishing, etc.?

Do you see yourself interacting much with others? Would you like to have these activities be organized? Are there vistas and horizons to gaze endlessly upon, or is there an abundance of visual activity and changing scenery?

Are you enjoying exotic foods elaborately displayed and available to you at your leisure? Are you testing out your sense of adventure on the local cuisine and dining hot spots? Are you eating fast foods and pizza in exchange for spending your time and money on other items and activities that make your vacation exciting?

Are your evenings filled with romantic strolls or festivities that run late into the night? Are you staying in for romantic evenings or re-energizing for another busy day of honeymooning?

HOW TO USE THIS WORKSHEET

Each of you separately should place a check mark next to the items or images on the wish list that appeal to you. After you have finished, highlight those items that both of you feel are important (the items that were checked by both of you).

Next, each of you should highlight, in a different colored marker or pen, 2-3 items in each category that you feel are very important to you individually (even though the other person may not have checked it.

Your wish lists, after completing this exercise, will probably look like a list of all of the positive elements of all of your dream vacations combined. This is good; you should list as many things as you can think of. The more information you have, the better the suggestions your travel agent (or yourself if you'll be doing your own research) will be able to make.

Together, using this wish list, you will discover a honeymoon destination and match a honeymoon style that will fulfill your dreams. The resource leads and exercises provided in the rest of this book will help you get from wish list to reality. Happy planning!

WISH LIST

LOCATION	BRIDE	GROOM
Hot Weather		
Mild Weather		
Cold Weather		
Dry Climate		
Moist Climate		
Sand and Beaches		
Lakes/Ponds		
Wilderness/Wooded Area		
Mountains		
Fields		
City Streets		
Small Local Town		
Large Metropolitan Area		
Popular Tourist Destination		
Visiting Among the Locals		
Nighttime Weather Conducive to Outdoor Activities		
Nighttime Weather Conducive to Indoor Activities		
"Modern" Resources and Service Available		
"Roughing It" On Your Own		
Culture and Customs You Are Familiar and Comfortable With		
New Cultures and Customs You Would Like to Get to Know		

ACCOMMODATIONS

	BRIDE	GROOM
Part of a Larger Resort Community		
A Stand-Alone Building		
Lodging Amongst Other Fellow Tourists		
Lodging Amongst Couples Only		
Lodging Amongst Fellow Newlyweds Only		

ACCOMMODATIONS

	BRIDE	GROOM
Lodging Amongst Locals		
Large Room or Suite		
Plush, Highly Decorated Surroundings		
Modestly Sized Room		
Modest Décor		
Balcony		
Private Jacuzzi in Room		
Room Service		
Chamber Maid Service		
Laundry/Dry Cleaning Service Available		
Laundry Room Available		
Beauty Salon on Premises		
Gym on Premises		
Gift Shop on Premises		
Pool on Premises		
Pool Side Bar Service		
Sauna, Hot Tub on Premises		
Common Gathering Lounge for Guests		

MEALS

	BRIDE	GROOM
Casual Dining		
Formal Dining		
Prepared by Executive Chefs		
Prepared by Yourself/Grocery Store		
Variety of Local and Regional Cuisine		
Traditional American Cuisine		
Opportunity for Picnics		
Exotic, International Menu		
Entertainment While Dining		

WISH LIST

MEALS	BRIDE	GROOM
Planned Meal Times		
Dining Based on Your Own Schedule		
Fast Food Restaurants		
Vegetarian/Special Diet Meals		
Delis, Diners		

ACTIVITIES

	BRIDE	GROOM
Sunbathing		
Snorkeling		
Diving		
Swimming		
Jet Skiing		
Water Skiing		
Fishing		
Sailing		
Snow Skiing		
Snowboarding		
Hiking/Rock Climbing		
Camping		
Golf		
Tennis		
Aerobics		
Sight-seeing Suggestions and Guidance		
Planned Bus/Guided Tours		
Ability to Go Off on Your Own		
Historic Tours		
Art Museums		
Theater		
Exploring Family Heritage		

NIGHTLIFE

	BRIDE	GROOM
Nightlife		
Quiet Strolls		
Outdoor Activities		
Sitting and Relaxing Outdoors		
Sitting and Relaxing in Front of a Fireplace		
Being Alone with Each Other		
Being Out with the Locals		
Being Out with Other Newlyweds		
Discovering New Cultures and Forms of Entertainment		
Dancing		
Visiting Bars/Pubs		
Theater/Shows		
Gambling		

OTHER IMPORTANT ELEMENTS

WISH LIST

CREATING A WISH LIST

Now that you have created a wish list, take this list to your travel agent. If you don't already have a travel agent, use the following section to select a reputable agent.

A good travel agent, especially one who works with a lot of honeymooners, will be able to tell you about several different places that match your wish list while staying within your budget. (The section entitled Creating a Budget will prove invaluable in determining exactly what your budget will be.) Your travel agent should be able to provide a variety of options which contain different combinations of the elements of your wish list. Discuss with him or her which "lower priority" items you are willing to forego in order to experience the best of your "top priorities."

HELPFUL RESOURCES

THE FOLLOWING PAGES INCLUDE HELPFUL RESOURCES that will come in handy when planning your honeymoon. Find information regarding travel agents and guidebooks, as well as websites and telephone numbers of travel bureaus from around the world.

TRAVEL AGENTS

Using the services of a good travel agent will take a lot of unnecessary pressure off of you. In the past, you may have felt you did not need the assistance of a travel agent when planning a vacation. Planning a honeymoon, however, can often be far more involved and stressful than a "regular" vacation, due to the simple fact that you are also deeply enmeshed in the planning of your wedding!

Therefore, you should take advantage of the professional resources available to you when working out the small details and finding the best values. Keep in mind, though, that you will still probably want to do some research on your own, ask for second opinions and, most of all, read the fine print.

Since a travel agent can become one of your most valuable resources, you will want to consider a few important things when trying to select one. Ask family, friends, and coworkers for personal recommendations (especially from former honeymooners). If you are unable to find an agent through a personal referral, then select a few agencies that are established nearby from newspapers, phone books, etc.

Next, you will want to make an appointment with an agent or speak to one over the phone. Pay close attention to the following and then make your decision.

Find out if they are a member of the American Society of Travel Agents (ASTA). Additionally, find out if they are also a Certified Travel Counselor (CTC), or possibly a Destination Specialist (DS).

ASTA: Members of this organization are required to have at least 5 years of travel agent experience. They also agree to adhere to strict codes and standards of

HELPFUL RESOURCES

integrity in travel issues as established by the national society. In most states, there are no formal regulations requiring certain qualifications for being a travel agent. In other words, any person can decide to call him/herself a travel agent.

CTC: Certified Travel Counselors have successfully completed a 2-year program in travel management.

DS: Destination Specialists have successfully completed studies focusing on a particular region of travel.

For a list of ASTA agencies in your area, call or write:

American Society of Travel Agents
Consumer Affairs Department
1101 King Street, Suite 200
Alexandria, VA 22314
(703) 739-2782
www.ASTAnet.com

For a list of Destination Specialists and Certified Travel Agents in your area, call or write:

Institute of Certified Travel Agents
148 Linden Street
P.O. Box 56
Wellesley, MA 02181
(800) 542-4282 (press "0" to be connected to a Travel Counselor)
www.ICTA.com

QUESTIONS TO QUALIFY YOUR TRAVEL AGENT:

- How long has the travel agency been in business?
- How long has the travel agent been with the agency?
- How much experience does the travel agent have? Any special studies or travels?
- Do they have a good resource library?
- Does the agent/agency have a variety of brochures to offer?
- Do they have travel videos to lend?
- Do they have a recommended reading list of travel aid books?

- Does the agent seem to understand your responses on your wish list and budget?

- Does he/she seem excited to help you?

- Does the agent listen carefully to your ideas? Take notes on your conversations? Ask you questions to ensure a full understanding?

- Is the agent able to offer a variety of different possibilities that suit your interests based on your wish list? Do the suggestions fall within your budget?

- Can the agent relay back to you (in his/her own words) what your wish list priorities are? What your budget priorities are?

- Is the agent prompt in getting back in touch with you?

- Is the agent reasonably quick in coming up with suggestions and alternatives? Are the suggestions exciting and within reason?

- Does the agent take notes on your interests (degree of sports, leisure, food, etc.)?

- Does the travel agency provide a 24 hour emergency help line?

- Are you documenting your conversations and getting all of your travel plans and reservations confirmed in writing?

Aside from just offering information and arrangements about locations and discounts, a good travel agent should also provide you with information about passports, customs, travel and health insurance, travelers' checks, and any other information important to a traveler.

OTHER SOURCES

National bridal magazines and general travel magazines are a great place to search for honeymoon ideas. But remember, you cannot always believe every word in paid advertising.

In addition to the information your travel agent provides, you can also obtain maps, brochures, and other useful items on your own. At the end of this section, you will find many useful phone numbers to help you in contacting tourist bureaus and travel agencies worldwide. These offices are extremely helpful in acquiring both general information (about weather, tourist attractions, landmarks, and even coupons or promotional brochures "selling" the area) and more specific information about reputable hotels, inns, bed and breakfasts, restaurants, etc.

HELPFUL RESOURCES

Also provided in this section are phone numbers for sources specializing in information about traveling by train (in the United States as well as abroad) and for camping and hiking throughout the country.

The internet, your local library, the travel section of book stores, and travel stores are excellent sources for finding information and tips relevant to your travel needs. You will find books on traveling in general as well as books specific to the region or destination you will be visiting. There are numerous tour books, maps, language books and tapes, as well as books about a location's culture, traditions, customs, climate, and geography.

These books are a great source of information since they are independent from the locations they describe and are therefore impartial, objective, and usually contain correct, unbiased information. You can also find books and other resources describing (and sometimes rating) restaurants, hotels, shows, and tours. Books on bargain hunting and finding the best deals are common as well.

SOURCES TO READ

- *The Ultimate Guide to the World's Best Wedding and Honeymoon Destinations*, written by Elizabeth & Alex Lluch. A comprehensive resource for planning your honeymoon, including information on popular destinations and information on hotels and resorts.

- The Stephen Birnbaum travel guides

- Frommer's guides

- Michelin Green Guides; Michelin Red Guides

- Insight Guides

- Let's Go! guides

- Fodor's guides

- Fielding's travel books

- *The New York Times Practical Traveler*

- *Mobil Travel Guide*

BACKGROUND NOTES

- **National Park Service Publications**
  (202) 208-4747
  www.nps.gov

- **National Forest Service Publications**
  (202) 205-8333
  A Guide to Your National Forests
  www.fs.fed.us

HELPFUL RESOURCES

STATE TOURISM BUREAUS

Alabama Bureau of Tourism	800-ALABAMA	www.touralabama.com
Alaska Travel Industry Association	907-929-2200	www.travelalaska.com
Arizona Office of Tourism	866-275-5816	www.arizonaguide.com
Arkansas Dept. of Parks and Tourism	800-NATURAL	www.arkansas.com
California Tourism Office	800-862-2543	www.gocalif.com
Colorado Tourism Board	800-COLORADO	www.colorado.com
Connecticut Vacation Center	800-CT-BOUND	www.ctbound.com
D.C. Convention and Visitors Association	202-789-7000	www.washington.org
Delaware Tourism Office	866-284-7483	www.visitdelaware.com
Visit Florida	850-488-5607	www.flausa.com
Georgia Department of Industry Trade	800-VISIT-GA	www.georgia.org
Hawaii Visitors & Convention Bureau	800-464-2924	www.hawaii.com
Idaho Division of Tourism Development	800-635-7820	www.visitid.org
Illinois Bureau of Tourism	800-2-CONNECT	www.enjoyillinois.com
Indiana Department of Commerce	888-ENJOY-IN	www.enjoyindiana.com
Iowa Tourism Office	888-472-6035	www.traveliowa.com
Kansas Department of Travel & Tourism	800-2-KANSAS	www.travelks.com
Kentucky Dept. of Travel Development	800-225-TRIP	www.kentuckytourism.com
Louisiana Office of Tourism	800-33-GUMBO	www.louisianatravel.com
Maine Bureau of Tourism	888-624-6345	www.visitmaine.com
Maryland Office of Tourist Development	800-MD-IS-FUN	www.mdisfun.org
Massachusetts Department of Tourism	800-447-MASS	www.massvacation.com
Michigan Department of Commerce	888-78-GREAT	www.michigan.org
Minnesota Office of Tourism	800-657-3700	www.exploreminnesota.com
Mississippi Office of Tourism	800-WARMEST	www.visitmississippi.org
Missouri Travel Center	800-877-1234	www.visitmo.com
Montana Travel Promotion Division	800-VISIT-MT	www.visitmt.com
Nebraska Dept. of Travel and Tourism	800-228-4307	www.visitnebraska.org
Nevada Commission on Tourism	800-NEVADA-8	www.travelnevada.com
New Hampshire Division of Tourism	800-FUN-IN-NH	www.visitnh.gov
New Jersey Office of Travel & Tourism	800-JERSEY-7	www.visitnj.org

New Mexico Department of Tourism ....800-SEE-NEWMEX ....www.newmexico.org

New York Division of Tourism ....800-CALL-NYS ....www.www.iloveny.com

North Carolina Travel & Tourism Division ....800-VISIT-NC..www.visitnc.com

North Dakota Tourism Division ....800-HELLO-ND.............................www.ndtourism.com

Ohio Department of Travel & Tourism ....800-BUCKEYE ....www.ohiotourism.com

Oklahoma Tourism and Recreation Dept.........................800-652-6552 ....www.travelok.com

Oregon Tourism Commission ....800-547-7842 .... www.traveloregon.com

Pennsylvania Department of Tourism ....800-VISIT-PA.............................www.experiencepa.com

Rhode Island Tourism Division..800-556-2484 .... www.visitrhodeisland.com

South Carolina Dept. of Parks, Recreation and Tourism .....800-346-3634.................www.discoversouthcarolina.com

South Dakota Division of Tourism....................................800-S-DAKOTA..www.travelsd.com

Tennessee Department of Tourism ....800-GO-2-TENN .... www.tnvacation.com

Texas Travel and Information Bureau ....800-888-8-TEX .... www.traveltex.com

Utah Travel Council..800-200-1160 ....www.utah.com

Vermont Travel Division ....800-VERMONT ....www.travel-vermont.com

Virginia Division of Tourism..800-VISIT-VA .... www.virginia.org

Washington Tourism Development ....800-544-1800 .... www.experiencewashington.com

West Virginia Div. of Tourism & Parks.............................800-CALL-WVA .... www.callwva.com

Wisconsin Division of Tourism ....800-432-TRIP...........................www.travelwisconsin.com

Wyoming Travel & Tourism ....800-CALL-WYO ....www.wyomingtourism.org

U.S. Virgin Islands Division of Tourism .... www.usvitourism.vi

INTERNATIONAL TOURISM BUREAUS

Anguilla Tourist Information ....800-553-4939 ....www.anguilla-vacation.com

Antigua Tourist Office ....212-541-4117 .... www.antigua-barbuda.org

Argentina Tourist Information ....800-722-5737.............www.turismo.gov.ar/eng/menu.htm

Aruba Tourism Authority...404-89-ARUBA ....www.aruba.com

Australian Tourist Commission.. www.australia.com

Austrian National Tourist Office ....www.austria-tourism.at

Bahamas Tourist Office..800-422-4262 .... www.bahamas.com

Balkan Holidays...800-822-1106 .... www.balkan-travel.com

HELPFUL RESOURCES

Barbados Board of Tourism .... 800-221-9831 .... www.barbados.org

Belgian Tourist Office .... 212-758-8130 .... www.visitbelgium.com

Belize Tourist Board .... 800-624-0686 .... travelbelize.org

Bermuda Department of Tourism .... 800-BERMUDA .... www.bermudatourism.com

Bonaire Tourist Information Office .... 800-BONAIRE .... www.infobonaire.com

Brazil Tourism Office .... 800-544-5503 .... www.brazilres.com

Visit Britain .... 800-462-2748 .... www.travelbritain.org

Canadian Consulate .... 613-946-1000 .... www.travelcanada.ca

    Alberta: .... 800-661-8888 .... www.travelalberta.com

    British Columbia: .... 800-HELLO-BC .... www.hellobc.com

    Manitoba: .... 800-665-0040 .... www.travelmanitoba.com

    New Brunswick: .... 800-561-0123 .... www.tourismnewbrunswick.ca

    Newfoundland: .... 800-563-6353 .... www.gov.nf.ca/tourism/

    Nova Scotia: .... 800-565-0000 .... www.explorens.com

    Ontario: .... 800-ONTARIO .... www.ontariotravel.net

    Prince Edward: .... 800-PEI-PLAY .... www.peiplay.com

    Quebec: .... 877-BONJOUR .... www.bonjourquebec.com

    Saskatchewan: .... 877-2-ESCAPE .... www.sasktourism.com

    Yukon: .... 867-667-5340 .... www.touryukon.com

Caribbean Tourism Organization .... 800-603-3545 .... www.doitcaribbean.com

Cayman Islands Department of Tourism .... 212-889-9009 .... www.caymanislands.ky

Chile National Tourist Board .... 800-244-5366 .... www.visitchile.com

China National Tourist Office .... 818-545-7505 .... www.cnto.org

Colombian Consulate .... 202-332-7476 .... www.colombiaemb.org

Cook Islands Tourist Authority .... 888-994-2665 .... www.cook-islands.com

Costa Rican Tourist Board .... 800-343-6332 .... www.visitcostarica.com

Curacao Tourist Board .... 800-683-7660 .... www.curacao-tourism.com

Cyprus Consulate General .... 212-683-5280 .... www.cyprustourism.org

CEDOK (Czech Republic and Slovakia) .... 212-288-0830 .... www.czechcenter.com

Denmark Tourist Board .... 212-885-9700 .... www.visitdenmark.com

Dominican Republic Tourist Info. Center .... 888-DR-INFO .... www.dominica.com.do

Egyptian Tourist Authority .... 312-280-4666 .... touregypt.net

Fiji Visitors Bureau .... 800-YEA-FIJI .... www.BulaFiji.com

Finland Tourist Board ....800-FIN-INFO................................... www.gofinland.org

French Government Tourist Office....................................410-286-8310 .... www.franceguide.com

French West Indies 877-956-1234

German National Tourist Office ....323-655-6085 .... www.visits-to-germany.com

Greece National Tourist Authority.....................................212-421-5777 .... www.greektourism.com

Grenada Department of Tourism ....212-687-9554 ....www.grenada.org

Guam Visitors Bureau ....800-US-3-GUAM .... www.visitguam.org

Guatemala Tourist Commission ....888-464-8281 .... www.guatemala.travel.com.gt

Honduras Tourist Bureau...800-410-9608 .... www.honduras.com

Hong Kong Tourist Association ....212-421-3382 .... www.discoverhongkong,com/usa/

Hungary Tourist Board ....212-355-0240 .... www.gotohungary.com

Iceland Tourist Board..212-885-9747 ....www.icetourist.is

India Tourist Office..800-953-9399 .... www.tourismindia.com

Indonesian Tourist Office..808-638-8500 .... www.indonesia2001.com

Ireland Tourist Board ....800-223-6470 .... www.tourismireland.com

Israeli Government Tourist Office...................................888-77-ISRAEL ....www.goisrael.com

Italian Tourist Office...212-245-4822 .... www.italiantourism.com

Jamaican Tourist Board..800-JAMAICA........................... www.jamaicatravel.com

Japan National Tourist Office...212-757-5640 .... www.japantravelinfo.com

Kenya Tourist Office ....202-387-6101 .... www.magicalkenya.com

Korea National Tourist Office ....800-868-7567 .... www.tour2korea.com

Luxembourg National Tourist Office ....212-935-8888 .... www.visitluxembourg.com

Macau Tourist Office...www.macautourism.gov.mo

Malaysian Tourist Centre..213-689-9702 .... www.tourismmalysia.com

Malta National Tourist Office ....212-430-3799 ....www.visitmalta.com

Mexican Tourist Office ....800-44-MEXICO........................... www.visitmexico.com

Monaco Government Tourist Office ....800-753-9696 .... www.visitmonaco.com

Morocco National Tourist Office...wwww.tourism-in-morocco.com

Netherlands Board of Tourism..416-363-1577 .... www.goholland.com

New Zealand Tourist Office ....800-NEW-ZEALAND....................www.newzealand.com

Norway Scandinavia Tourist Offices....................................212-421-7333 ....www.norway.org

Papua/New Guinea Tourist Office ....949-752-5440 ....www.pngtourism.org.pg

Philippine Department of Tourism ....213-487-4525 .... wowphilippines.com.ph

HELPFUL RESOURCES

Poland National Tourism Office ....201-420-3370 .... www.polandtour.org

Portugal National Tourist Office.......................................212-354-4403 .... www.portugal.org

Puerto Rico Tourism Office ....800-866-STAR ....www.gotopuertorico.com,

Romanian National Tourist Office....................................212-545-8484 ....www.romaniatourism.com

Russian Travel Information Office ....877-221-7120 ....www.russia-travel.com

Singapore Tourist Board...323-852-1901 .... www.singapore-usa.com

South African Tourism Board ....800-822-5368 ....www.satour.org

Spain National Tourism Office ....212-265-8822 .... www.okspain.org

Sri Lanka Tourist Board..202-483-4025 ....www.slembassyusa.org

St. Kitts Tourist Board ....212-535-1234 .... www.stkittsnevis.org

St. Lucia Tourist Board ....800-4-ST-LUCIA .... www.stlucia.org

St. Maarten Tourist Office ....800-786-2278 .... www.st-maarten.com

St. Vincent/Grenadines Tourist Office ....212-687-4981 ....www.svgtourism.com

Sweden Travel & Tourism Board ....212-885-9700 ....www.visit-sweden.com

Switzerland National Tourist Office....................................877-SWITZERLAND .... www.myswitzerland.com

Tahitian Tourist Board ....310-414-8484 ....www.tahiti-tourisme.com

Taiwan Visitors Association ....212-867-1632 .... www.taiwan.net.tw

Thailand Tourism Authority ....212-432-0433 ....www.tourismthailand.org

Trinidad and Tobago Tourist Board... www.visitTNT.com

Tunisian Tourist Office ....202-862-1850 ....www.tourismtunisia.com

Turkish Tourism Office ....212-687-2194 .... www.tourismturkey.org

Venezuela Tourism Association ....415-331-0100 ....www.venezuela.com

OTHER TOURISM BUREAUS AND SERVICES

National Park Service...202-208-4747 .... www.nps.gov

American Automobile Association ....407-444-8000 .... www.aaa.com

Amtrak National Railroad Passenger Info. ....800-872-7245 ....www.amtrak.com

Rail Europe ....800-438-7245 ....www.raileurope.com

Via Rail Canada..800-561-3949 ....www.viarail.ca

CREATING A BUDGET

YOU WANT YOUR HONEYMOON TO GIVE YOU LUXURIOUS EXPERIENCES and price-less memories. But you don't want to return from your vacation faced with debts and unnecessary feelings of guilt for not having stayed within a reasonable budget. This should be the vacation of a lifetime. You can make this trip into anything your imagination allows. Pay attention to which experiences or details you would consider a "must have" and prioritize from there.

As you work with your budget, stay focused on those top priority items and allow less "elaborate" solutions for lower priority items. If you stay true to your most important vacation objectives, the minor sacrifices along the way will barely be noticed.

Perhaps, at this point, you don't know how many days your honeymoon will last. Often, the number of days you'll vacation depends on the type of honeymoon you choose. If you (and your travel agent) are designing your own honeymoon, the typical cost-per-day will most likely determine your length of stay. If you opt for a cruise or another type of prearranged vacation, your length of stay will probably be dependent upon the designated length of the travel package. By determining a basic, overall budget at the start, you will know what your limits are.

Yes, this is a very romantic time ... but try to remain realistic! Once you have an idea of your spending limits, your choices will be much easier to make.

Don't be discouraged if you're unable to spend an infinite amount of money on this trip. Very few couples are able to live life so carefree. You can still experience a honeymoon that will leave you filled with those priceless memories ... it's all in the planning!

The following budget worksheets will help guide you in creating your honeymoon budget. You may want to make copies of this worksheet so that you can create several budget plans. Keep trying different variations until you are satisfied with how your expenses will be allocated.

CREATING A BUDGET

When comparing your potential honeymoon options, you'll find that laying out a simple budget is an effective and essential tool for making decisions.

GENERAL BUDGET

Traditionally the groom is responsible for the honeymoon. The groom will take on the challenges of gathering information and working through the necessary details of providing a perfect honeymoon for his new bride ... and himself! Nowadays, many couples find it necessary for both the bride and groom to contribute to the cost in order to experience the honeymoon of their dreams. (Today, the average newlywed couple spends $2,500-$3,500 on their honeymoon.) Many couples, together, determine what each partner will contribute and then shape the budget from there.

Some couples find that including the suggestion of a "Money Contribution Toward a Memorable Honeymoon" as a gift in their bridal registry is a great way for friends and family to contribute to the trip. Some couples also include some version of a "Dollar Dance" at their reception. This is a great way for the bride and groom to dance with many of their guests while accepting the dollar "dance fee" as a contribution to their honeymoon. Some couples choose to pursue less romantic options for building up the honeymoon savings ... part-time jobs, yard sales, etc.

Whatever your methods may be, remember that increasing the amount of money you will spend does not automatically ensure a more pleasurable and enjoyable vacation. Your most important and effective resource is your commitment to planning. You will see that, regardless of what your budget limits may be, your vacation possibilities are endless.

Note: Even if you think you have a good sense of what you will spend (or even if you plan on going with an all-inclusive package) going through this exercise is a smart way to ensure that there will be no surprises later on.

GENERAL BUDGET

Amount from the wedding budget set
aside for the honeymoon:

$ _____

Amount groom is able to contribute from
current funds/savings:

$ _____

Amount bride is able to contribute from
current funds/savings:

$ _____

Amount to be saved/acquired by groom from
now until the honeymoon date (monthly
contributions, part-time job, gifts, bonuses):

$ _____

Amount to be saved/acquired by bride from
now until the honeymoon date (monthly
contributions, part-time job, gifts, bonuses):

$ _____

General Budget Total Amount:

$ _____

CREATING A BUDGET

DETAILED BUDGET

BEFORE THE HONEYMOON

Special honeymoon clothing purchases: $ _____

Bride's trousseau (honeymoon lingerie): $ _____

Sundries (**Helpful Hint:** Make a list of what you $ _____
already have and what you need to purchase.
You can then use these lists as part of your packing list. See Packing Checklist.):

Film, disposable cameras, extra camera batteries: $ _____

Maps, guidebooks, travel magazines: $ _____

Foreign language books and tapes, $ _____
translation dictionary:

Passport photos, application fees $ _____
(see International Travel):

Medical exam, inoculations $ _____
(see International Travel):

Other items: $ _____

Before the Honeymoon Total Amount:

$ _____

DETAILED BUDGET

DURING THE HONEYMOON

TRANSPORTATION

Airplane tickets: $ _____

Shuttle or cab (to and from the airport): $ _____

Car rental, gasoline, tolls: $ _____

Taxis, buses, other public transportation: $ _____

Transportation Total Amount:

$ _____

ACCOMMODATIONS

Hotel/resort room (total for entire stay): $ _____

Room service: $ _____

Miscellaneous "hidden costs" (Phone use, room taxes and surcharges, chambermaid and room service tips, in-room liquor bar and snacks): $ _____

Accommodations Total Amount:

$ _____

CREATING A BUDGET

DETAILED BUDGET

DURING THE HONEYMOON

MEALS

Breakfast: $ _____ per meal x _____ # of days = $ _____

Lunch: $ _____ per meal x _____ # of days = $ _____

Casual Dinners: $ _____ per meal x _____ # of days = $ _____

Formal Dinners: $ _____ per meal x _____ # of days = $ _____

Picnics, Snacks: $ _____ per meal x _____ # of days = $ _____

Meals Total Amount:

$ _____

ENTERTAINMENT

Sport and activity lessons $ _____
(tennis, golf, ballroom dancing, etc.):

Day excursions and tours $ _____
(boat tours, diving, snorkeling,
bus/guided tours, etc.):

Shows, theater: $ _____

Lounges, nightclubs, discos $ _____
(don't forget to include the cost
of drinks and bar gratuities):

Museum fees: $ _____

Pampering $ _____
(massages, spa treatments, hairdresser, etc.):

Entertainment Total Amount:

$ _____

MISCELLANEOUS

Souvenirs for yourselves: $ _____

Souvenirs and gifts for family and friends: $ _____

Postcards (including cost of stamps): $ _____

Newspapers and magazines: $ _____

Additional film, replacement sundries, other: $ _____

Miscellaneous Total Amount:

$ _____

CREATING A BUDGET

DETAILED BUDGET

AFTER THE HONEYMOON

Film developing costs: $ _____

Photo albums: $ _____

After the Honeymoon Total Amount:

$ _____

FOR ALL-INCLUSIVE RESORTS/CRUISES AND TRAVEL PACKAGES ONLY

Fill in the entire budget form above (simply put a $0.00 on the items to be included in the total package price). Then list the total inclusive package price on the line below. Don't forget to include taxes and surcharges.

Inclusive Package Price: $ _____

Detailed Budget Total Amount:

$ _____

Doing a budget analysis may be one of the most useful things you can do in planning your honeymoon. With all the options available, a good cost analysis will help make the most appropriate decisions very clear to you.

First, create a budget using the above worksheet for what you think allows for an ideal, yet reasonable, honeymoon. Highlight those expenses which are top priorities. For example, a spacious, ritzy hotel room may be the most important element for you. Or, perhaps participating in numerous sports activities and excursions or enjoying fine dining is more important than a spacious room.

Next, as you come across different destinations and options that appeal to you, fill in a new budget worksheet. Compare the results to other potential trips. See how your priority items on each trip compare to one another. Determine the pros and cons of each. This is also an effective way of looking at the pros and cons of an all-inclusive package versus an independently organized trip.

Note: Once you've decided on your honeymoon destination and activities, fill in a new budget as accurately as possible and take it with you on your trip. Use it to chart your expenses as they occur so you will have a visual guide of whether or not you are staying within budget.

If you find that you are going over your budget, take a look at those top priority items that you'd still like to keep. See if you can eliminate some lower priority items to free up some money for the favored ones.

If you find you are under budget, celebrate with a special "gift" for yourselves (massages, an extravagant dinner, another afternoon of jet skiing, etc.).

NOTES

TIPPING GUIDE

THIS GUIDE IS PROVIDED TO HELP YOU GET FAMILIAR WITH CUSTOMARY gratuity standards you may encounter throughout your travels.

Tipping customs vary from country to country. It is advisable to inquire about tipping with the international tourism board representing the country you'll be traveling in. Simply ask for information about tipping customs and social expectations. You will also want to discuss gratuities with your travel agent or planner. Some travel packages include gratuities in the total cost, some leave that to the guests, and some even discourage tipping (usually because they have built it into the total package price). Be sure to discuss this with your travel planner.

SERVICE	GRATUITY
AIR TRAVEL	
Skycaps	$1.00 per bag
Flight Attendants	None
ROAD TRAVEL	
Taxi Drivers	15% of fare (no less than 50 cents)
Limousine Driver	15%
Valet Parking	$1.00
Tour Bus Guide	$1.00
RAIL TRAVEL	
Redcaps	$1.00 per bag (or posted rate plus 50 cents)
Sleeping Car Attendant	$1.00 per person
Train Conductor & Crew	none
Dining Car Attendant	15% of bill

TIPPING GUIDE

SERVICE   **GRATUITY**

CRUISE

Cabin Steward ....$3 per person per day
Dining Room Waiter...$3 per person per day
Busboy ....$1.50 per person per day
Maitre d' ....At your discretion—recommended $10 - $20
Salon or Spa Personnel..15%
Bartender ....$1 - $2 per drink

RESTAURANTS

Maitre d', Head Waiter ....None (Unless special services provided, then typically $5.00)
Waiter/Waitress .... 15% of bill (pretax total)
Bartender ....$1 - $2 per drink
Wine Steward.. 15% of bill
Washroom Attendant...$.50 - $1.00
Coat Check Attendant .... $1.00 per coat
Note: Some restaurants in foreign countries add the gratuity and/or service charge to your bill.
If it has not been added, tip the customary regional rate.

HOTEL/RESORT

Concierge ....$2.00 - $10.00 for special attention or arrangements
Doorman..$1.00 for hailing taxi
Bellhop..$1.00 per bag + $1.00 for showing room
Room Service .... 15% of bill
Chamber Maid...................................$1.00 - $2.00 per day or $5.00 - $10.00 per week for longer stays
(no tip for one-night stays)
Pool Attendant... $.50 for towel service

MISCELLANEOUS

Barbershop...15% of cost
Beauty Salon ....15% of cost
Manicure...$1.00 - $5.00 depending on cost of service
Facial ....15% of cost
Massage ....15% of cost

THINGS TO PACK

CONSIDER THE DIFFERENCES IN THE CLIMATES of where you live now and where you'll be visiting. Also consider the air conditions of airplanes, trains and boats. Bring along items that will help in the transition and keep you feeling as comfortable as possible.

TRAVELERS' FIRST AID KIT

- ❐ Aspirin
- ❐ Antacid tablets
- ❐ Diarrhea medication
- ❐ Cold remedies/sinus decongestant
- ❐ Throat lozenges
- ❐ Antiseptic lotion
- ❐ Band-Aids
- ❐ Moleskin for blisters
- ❐ Breath mints
- ❐ Chapstick
- ❐ Insect repellent, insect bite medication
- ❐ Sunblock and sunburn relief lotion
- ❐ Dry skin lotion/hand cream
- ❐ Eye drops or eye lubricant
- ❐ Saline nasal spray, moisturizing nasal spray
- ❐ Vitamins
- ❐ Prescription drugs

  Note: These should be kept in their original pharmacy containers that provide both drug and doctor information. Be sure to note the drug's generic name. You will want to pack these in your carry-on baggage in case the bags you've checked become lost or delayed.

- ❐ Prescription or other birth control
- ❐ Physicians' names, addresses, and telephone numbers
- ❐ Health insurance phone numbers

  Note: Be sure to contact your provider to find out about coverage while traveling in the U.S. and abroad.

- ❐ Names and phone numbers of people to contact in case of an emergency

THINGS TO PACK

PACKING CHECKLIST

CARRY-ON BAGGAGE

- ❏ Travelers' First Aid Kit (see previous section)
- ❏ Wallet (credit cards, traveler's checks)
- ❏ Jewelry and other sentimental and valuable items that you feel you must bring
- ❏ Identification (passport, driver's license or photo ID)
- ❏ Photocopies of the following important documents:
- ❏ Hotel/resort street address, phone number, written confirmation of arrangements and reservations
- ❏ Complete travel itinerary
- ❏ Airline tickets
- ❏ Name, address and phone number of emergency contact person(s) back home
- ❏ Medicine prescriptions (including generic names) and eyeglass prescription information (or an extra pair); list of food and drug allergies
- ❏ Phone numbers (including after-hour emergency phone numbers) for health insurance company and personal physicians
- ❏ Copy of your packing list. This will help you while packing up at the end of your trip. It will also be invaluable if a piece of your luggage gets lost, as you will know the contents that are missing.
- ❏ List of your traveler's checks' serial numbers and 24-hour phone number for reporting loss or theft
- ❏ Phone numbers to the local U.S. embassy or consulate
- ❏ Any "essential" toiletries and one complete casual outfit in case checked baggage is delayed or lost
- ❏ Foreign language dictionary or translator
- ❏ Camera with film loaded
- ❏ Maps
- ❏ Small bills/change (in U.S. dollars and in the appropriate foreign currency) for tipping
- ❏ Currency converter chart or pocket calculator
- ❏ Reading material

CARRY-ON BAGGAGE (CONT.)

- ❑ Eyeglasses
- ❑ Contact lenses
- ❑ Contact lens cleaner
- ❑ Sunglasses
- ❑ Kleenex, gum, breath mints, and any over-the-counter medicine to ease travel discomfort
- ❑ Inflatable neck pillow (for lengthy travel)
- ❑ Address book and thank you notes (in case you have lots of traveling time)
- ❑ This book
- ❑ Your Budget Sheet

Other items to carry on

- ❑ _____
- ❑ _____
- ❑ _____
- ❑ _____
- ❑ _____

CHECKED BAGGAGE

CLOTHING

Casual Wear
Consider the total number of each casual outfit item that you will need.

- ❑ shorts
- ❑ pants
- ❑ tops
- ❑ jackets/sweaters
- ❑ sweatshirts/sweatsuits
- ❑ belts
- ❑ socks
- ❑ underwear/panties & bras
- ❑ walking shoes/sandals/loafers

THINGS TO PACK

❑ _____
❑ _____
❑ _____

Athletic Wear

Consider the total number of each sporting outfit item that you will need.

❑ shorts
❑ sweatpants
❑ tops
❑ sweatshirts/jackets
❑ swimsuits, swimsuit cover-up
❑ aerobic activity outfit
❑ athletic equipment
❑ socks
❑ underwear/panties & exercise bras
❑ tennis/athletic shoes

❑ _____
❑ _____
❑ _____

Evening Wear

Consider the total number of each evening outfit item that you will need.

❑ pants or pants/skirts/dresses
❑ belts
❑ dress shirts/blouses
❑ sweaters
❑ jackets/blazers/ties
❑ socks or pantyhose/slips
❑ underwear/panties & bras
❑ accessories/jewelry
❑ shoes

❑ _____
❑ _____
❑ _____

Formal Wear

Consider the number of each formal outfit item that you will need.

❑ dress pants/suits/tuxedo
❑ dresses/gowns
❑ accessories/jewelry
❑ socks or pantyhose/slips
❑ underwear/panties & bras
❑ dress shoes

❑ _____
❑ _____
❑ _____

Other clothing items

❑ pajamas
❑ lingerie
❑ slippers
❑ robe

❑ _____
❑ _____
❑ _____

MISCELLANEOUS ITEMS

❑ An additional set of the important document photocopies as packed in your carry-on bag
❑ Travel tour books, tourism bureau information numbers
❑ Journal
❑ Special honeymoon gift for your new spouse
❑ Any romantic items or favorite accessories
❑ Extra film and camera batteries
❑ Plastic bags for dirty laundry
❑ Large plastic or nylon tote bag for bringing home new purchases
❑ Small sewing kit and safety pins
❑ Travel alarm clock
❑ Travel iron, lint brush

THINGS TO PACK

- ❑ Compact umbrella, fold-up rain slickers
- ❑ Handheld tape recorder (for recorded memory journal or for bringing along your favorite, romantic tapes)
- ❑ Video camera

- ❑ _____
- ❑ _____
- ❑ _____

FOR INTERNATIONAL TRAVEL

- ❑ Passports/visas
- ❑ Electric converters and adapter plugs
- ❑ Copy of appropriate forms showing proof of required vaccinations/inoculations

OTHER ITEMS TO BRING

- ❑ _____
- ❑ _____
- ❑ _____
- ❑ _____
- ❑ _____

ITEMS TO LEAVE BEHIND *with a trusted contact person*

- ❑ Photocopy of all travel details (complete itineraries, names, addresses, and telephone numbers)
- ❑ Photocopy of credit cards along with 24-hour telephone number to report loss or theft. (Be sure to get the number to call when traveling abroad. It will be a different number than their U.S. 1-800 number.)
- ❑ Photocopy of traveler's checks along with 24-hour telephone number to report loss or theft
- ❑ Photocopy of passport identification page, along with date and place of issuance
- ❑ Photocopy of drivers license
- ❑ Any irreplaceable items

INTERNATIONAL TRAVEL

THERE ARE OVER 250 U.S. EMBASSIES AND CONSULATES around the world. After contacting the Tourism Bureau for the area you will be traveling to, it is also a wise idea to contact the U.S. Embassy or Consulate for that region. With assistance from both of these sources you will be able to determine the travel requirements and recommendations for your chosen travel destination. Within this section you will find numerous resources to assure all of your questions and concerns are addressed before you travel. Call for a list of U.S. embassy and consulate locations with emergency phone numbers: (202) 647-5225 or visit http://travel.state.gov

PASSPORTS AND VISAS

Your travel agent should be able to provide you with information to adequately prepare you for your international travels. Additional information (and possibly more detailed and current information) can be obtained by contacting the appropriate sources listed in this section.

As a U.S. citizen, you generally need a passport to enter and to depart most foreign countries and to reenter the United States. Some countries also require visas. A visa is an endorsement by officials of a foreign country as permission to visit their country. You first need a passport in order to obtain a visa. Inquire with the resources listed in this section for requirements of your specific destination.

As mentioned, you will be required to prove your U.S. citizenship upon reentry to the United States. If the country of your destination does not require you to possess a current passport, you will still need to produce proof of citizenship for U.S. Immigration. Items that are acceptable as proof of citizenship include a passport, a certified copy of your birth certificate, Certificate of Nationalization, a Certificate of Citizenship, or a Report of Birth Abroad of a Citizen of the United States. Proof of identification can include a driver's license or a government or military identification card containing a photo or physical description.

INTERNATIONAL TRAVEL

Note: The bride should have her passport and airline tickets reflect her maiden name for ease in proof of identification while traveling. Name changes can be processed after returning from the honeymoon with your marriage certificate.

Your passport will be one of the most important documents you will take with you. Contact the local U.S. Embassy immediately if your passport becomes lost or stolen. Have a photocopy of your passport's data page, date and place of issuance, and passport number to be kept with a contact person at home. You should also travel with a set of these photocopies in addition to an extra set of loose passport photos for speed in attaining a replacement.

Passports can be obtained from one of the 13 U.S. Passport Agencies (listed later in this section) or one of the thousands of authorized passport locations, such as state and federal courts as well as some U.S. Post Offices (check in the Government Listings section of your phone book).

Currently, the cost to obtain a passport is $65.00 (in person; Form DSP-11) or $55.00 (through the mail; Form DSP-82). If you have had a passport in the past, contact a passport agency to find out if you are eligible to apply through the mail. You will want to apply for your passport several months before your trip, keeping in mind that January through July is a busier time and the process may take longer.

In addition to calling the U.S. Passport Agencies for personal assistance, you can also call their 24-hour recorded information lines for information on agency locations, travel advisories and warnings, and Consular Information Sheets pertaining to every country in the world.

Travel Advisory Updates are also available 24 hours a day by calling The Department of State's Office of Overseas Citizens' Services at (202) 647-5225.

Additional, and very helpful, official information for U.S. citizens regarding international travel can be found at http://travel.state.gov.

Foreign embassies and consulates located in the U.S. can provide current information regarding their country. You can locate phone numbers and addresses in The Congressional Directory or Foreign Consular Offices in the United States, both available at your local library.

UNITED STATES PASSPORT AGENCIES

http://travel.state.gov/passport_services.html   For all inquiries, call............................... 800-688-9889

Boston Passport Agency

Thomas P. O'Neil Federal Building
Room 247, 10 Causeway Street
Boston, Massachusetts 02222-1094

Chicago Passport Agency

Kluczynski Federal Building
Suite 380, 230 South Dearborn Street
Chicago, Illinois 60604-1564

Honolulu Passport Agency

First Hawaii Tower
1132 Bishop St., Suite 500
Honolulu, Hawaii 96813-2809

Houston Passport Agency

Mickey Leland Federal Building
1919 Smith Street, Suite 1100
Houston, Texas 77002-8049

Los Angeles Passport Agency

11000 Wilshire Blvd., Room 13100
Los Angeles, California 90024-3615

Miami Passport Agency

Claude Pepper Federal Office Building, 3rd Floor
51 Southwest First Avenue
Miami, Florida 33130-1680

New Orleans Passport Agency

Postal Services Building, Room T-12005
701 Loyola Avenue
New Orleans, Louisiana 70113-1931

New York Passport Agency

Rockefeller Center, Room 270
630 Fifth Avenue
New York, New York 10111-0031

Philadelphia Passport Agency

U.S. Customs House
200 Chestnut Street Room 103
Philadelphia, Pennsylvania 19106-2970

San Francisco Passport Agency

555 Montgomery
San Francisco, California 94101

INTERNATIONAL TRAVEL

Seattle Passport Agency   Federal Office Building, Room 992
                                             915 Second Avenue
                                             Seattle, Washington 98174-1091

Stamford Passport Agency   One Landmark Square
                                             Broad and Atlantic Streets
                                             Stamford, Connecticut 06901-2667

Washington Passport Agency   1111 19th Street, N.W.
                                             Washington, D.C. 20522-1705

Some private sources offering assistance in obtaining a passport (usually with expedited service).

International Visa Service.. 800-627-1112
World Wide Visas 800-527-1861
Travel Document Systems .... 800-874-5100 or www.traveldocs.com

HEALTH CONCERNS

In the United States, the National Center for Infectious Diseases (NCID) and the Centers for Disease Control and Prevention (CDC) provide the most current information pertinent to international travel. The World Health Organization (WHO) concerns itself with general and specific health issues for almost every part of the world. Health and safety issues as related to international travel are the basis for the International Heath Regulations adopted by the World Health Organization.

Your travel agent should be fully informed about current conditions and requirements. Your personal physician should also be able to provide you with health-related information and advice for traveling in the region you visit. You can personally obtain very useful (and very thorough) information from the Centers for Disease Control and Prevention (CDC). The CDC's Travelers' Health Section has the following useful resources:

The Yellow Book, Health Information for International Travel
Order online at www.cdc.gov/travel/yb/

For updates and changes by phone or fax, call (404) 332-4559 or visit www.cdc.gov.

OTHER CONCERNS

TRAVELERS' HEALTH INSURANCE COVERAGE

If your health insurance policy does not cover you abroad, consider acquiring a temporary health insurance policy. Travel agencies, health insurance companies, traveler's check companies, and your local phone book should be able to provide names of relevant companies for you. In addition to health insurance coverage, many policy packages include protection in case of trip cancellation and baggage loss.

Keep prescription medications in their original pharmacy containers with the original labels. Bring a copy of your prescriptions and note the drug's generic name. You may consider getting a letter from your physician warranting your need for the medication.

CUSTOMS

The following list contains some useful publications regarding customs and custom policies when traveling internationally:

Know Before You Go: U.S. Customs and Border Protection Regulations for U.S. Residents
   U.S. Customs and Border Protection
   Available online at www.cbp.gov

An Unwanted Souvenir: Lead in Ceramic Ware
   U.S. Food and Drug Administration
   Available online at www.fda.gov

Buyer Beware
A brochure from the World Wildlife Fund and the U.S. Fish and Wildlife Service that addresses international products made from endangered or threatened wildlife.
   Available online at www.worldwildlife.org

NOTES

WE WOULD GREATLY APPRECIATE your writing us after your honeymoon to let us know how your wedding went and how much the *Easy Wedding Planning Plus* helped you in planning your event. We will use this information to continue improving this extensive wedding planner, and we may even use your story in our upcoming book about wedding experiences if you permit us to. We might even ask you to participate in some of our future radio and TV tours where you can tell your own story to the public! Feel free to use additional sheets, if necessary.

Dear Elizabeth & Alex,

I want to tell you that *Easy Wedding Planning Plus* (helped a lot), (helped a little) in planning my wedding. I especially liked your section on_____. My wedding was on_____, and it was (a complete success), (a wild party), (a boring event), (a complete disaster), (the most stressful day of my life).

My comments about your book are:
_____
_____
_____

I wish your book had given me information about:
_____
_____
_____

The best thing about my wedding was:
_____
_____
_____

The worst thing about my wedding was:
_____
_____
_____

TELL US ABOUT YOUR WEDDING

The funniest thing about my wedding was:

_____

_____

_____

What made my wedding special or unique was:

_____

_____

_____

My wedding would have been much better if:

_____

_____

_____

This is to authorize WS Publishing Group to use our story in any of their upcoming books. WS Publishing Group (can), (cannot) use our name when telling our story. I also (am), (am not) interested in participating in a radio/TV interview tour.

Bride's Name: _____   Bride's Signature: _____

Groom's Name: _____   Groom's Signature: _____

Address: _____

Home Number: _____   Work Number: _____

E-mail: _____

Fold in three and mail to WS Publishing Group.

Place
Stamp
Here

WS Publishing Group
7290 Navajo Road
Suite 207
San Diego, California 92119

WeddingSolutions.com

At the touch of love... 1004 d... **$99 Value**

AT THE TOUCH OF LOVE, EVERYONE BECOMES A POET. – PLATO

celebrating the wedding of
Sarah Jang & Christopher Smith
June 11, 2006

Us at a Glance

Bride: Sarah Sun-Wha Jang
Nickname: Damage Control
Occupation: Artist/Designer

Groom: Christopher Thomas Smith
Nickname: Damage
Occupation: Finance Manager

Dating for: 3 years
Engaged for: 1 year
Our Favorite Acivity: Eating out at yummy
restaurants. Anything that involves being together.

FREE Wedding Website on WeddingSolutions.com

Includes 19 Custom Pages

- Home
- Our Story
- Photo Gallery
- Details of Events
- Wedding Party
- Registry
- Local Info
- City Guide
- Accommodations
- Things to Do

- Restaurants
- Guest Book
- View Guest Book
- Sign Guest Book
- Wedding Journal
- Honeymoon
- Miscellaneous
- RSVP
- Contact Us
- Much More

SAVE UP TO $200 ON WEDDING INVITATIONS & ACCESSORIES

Invitations........................

SAVE up to $100

- Wedding Invitations
- Engagement
- Bridal Shower
- Rehearsal Dinner
- Casual Wedding
- Seal 'n Send
- Save The Date
- Maps/Direction Cards
- Programs
- Thank-You Notes
- Much More!

Accessories..........................

SAVE up to $100

- Toasting Glasses
- Attendants' Gifts
- Unity Candles
- Aisle Runners
- Cake Tops
- Flower Girl Basket
- Ring Pillow
- Guest Book
- Cake Knife & Server
- Favors
- Much More!

Log on to www.WeddingSolutions.com/specialoffers for more details on these offers

ULTIMATEREGISTRY.COM

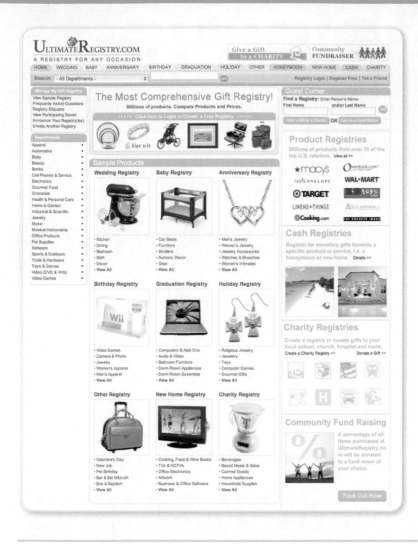

Create a gift registry for any occasion!

Choose from over one million products from the top U.S. merchants

- Gifts from the top U.S. merchants

- Compare products and prices

- Simplified notification process saves you time

- Same Merchants, Same Products, 1 Registry!

Already have everything you need or want?

Help those in need through our Charity Registry

Request that your guests donate much-needed products to the charity of your choice in lieu of wedding gifts.

"Give a Gift" allows your guests to donate much-needed products to the charity of your choice.

Your guests will be able to select from hundreds of national and local charities and see their "wish list" of items they need most, such as blankets, office supplies and more.

Your guests can then purchase these products in your name and they will be sent directly to the charity of your choice.

Log on to www.UltimateRegistry.com for more information